INTERVIEWS WITH MASTER PHOTOGRAPHERS

James Danziger and Barnaby Conrad III

INTERVIEWS WITH MASTER PHOTOGRAPHERS

Minor White
Imogen Cunningham
Cornell Capa
Elliott Erwitt
Yousuf Karsh
Arnold Newman
Lord Snowdon
Brett Weston

PADDINGTON
PRESS LTD
NEW YORK & LONDON

Library of Congress Cataloging in Publication Data

Danziger, James, 1953–
   Interviews with master photographers.

    1. Photographers—Interviews. I. Conrad,
Barnaby, 1953–   joint author. II. Title.
TR139.D36   770'.92'2 [B]   76-53315
ISBN 0-448-22183-7

Filmset and printed in England by
BAS Printers Limited, Wallop, Hampshire
Bound by Kitcat Ltd., London
Designed by Colin Lewis

IN THE UNITED STATES
PADDINGTON PRESS LTD.
Distributed by
GROSSET & DUNLAP

IN THE UNITED KINGDOM
PADDINGTON PRESS LTD.

IN CANADA
Distributed by
RANDOM HOUSE OF CANADA LTD.

IN AUSTRALIA
Distributed by
ANGUS & ROBERTSON PTY. LTD.

*To the photographers who gave so much of
their time and selves to be interviewed,
this book is respectfully dedicated.*

The authors would like to thank Lucinda Bunnen, Dick Ehrlich, Dorothy Everard, Lee Jones, and Leslie Redlich for their assistance; Doug Beube, Isabel Cazalet, Abe Frajndlich, and David Moroni for their kindness; and above all, Bhupendra Karia for his advice and encouragement.

Contents

Black and white plates fall between pages 96–97

INTRODUCTION

In January, 1975, when we first had the idea of doing a book of interviews with photographers, several new developments suggested that photography had at last emerged from the support of a small but dedicated circle to achieve a greater public acceptance. Among these developments were the step into the fine art market, the consistent inclusion of photography in the collections of museums and art galleries, and the establishment of independent photographic centers for both exhibition and sale. With the new economic realities (photographs reaching over $10,000 at auction) and the death of some of the leading figures of the first generation of modern photography—Walker Evans, Wynn Bullock, Edward Steichen—a new awareness of the history and future of photography was created. But in spite of this, photography remained an enigma to the general public.

A recurring question that seemed to be dominating the popular media's consideration of photography at the time was "Is Photography Art?" This is a question emblematic of the difficulties most people have in understanding modern photography, for while it is not entirely invalid, it is misdirected in the attention it draws away from the finished work to the medium itself. To better understand photography, what was needed at this time was a closer focus on the individuals who take the photographs and the photographs themselves.

Rather than being overly concerned with technical details, the following interviews deal more specifically with the ideas behind the individual photographer's work. In my introductory letter to the different photographers, I described the aim of the interviews as being to find out "how photographers see their work and how they would like their work to be seen"; this remains a fair summation of the book's intent.

The eight interviews were conducted between January and September, 1976. They were taped, transcribed, edited, and sent to the photographers for final approval.

The photographers were chosen for the important positions they held in relation to all fields of contemporary photography. Photojournalists, portraitists, photographers of landscape and nature—what they have in common is the ability to use the medium of photography for their individual expressive purposes. This ability and the consistency of their achievement are what make them the masters of modern photography.

James Danziger
London. October, 1976

Minor White

Minor White was born in Minneapolis, Minnesota, in 1908. He studied Botany and English at the University of Minnesota, and although photography was a hobby of his from an early age, he concentrated on writing poetry until the middle thirties. In 1937 he began taking documentary photographs of the architecture around Portland, Oregon, and one year later he was appointed a "creative photographer" for the Works Progress Administration—a program established by Franklin Roosevelt to help artists caught without funds by the Depression.

In 1940 White became a teacher at the Le Grande Art Center in Oregon, and around this time, he began experimenting with the sequencing of photographs, presenting a group of photographs in which, in his own words, "the meaning appears in the space between the images, in the mood they raise in the beholder."

In 1942 White was drafted into the army, and shortly afterwards he was baptized into the Catholic Church. He left the army in 1945 and came to New York to study museum methodology with Beaumont and Nancy Newhall, the prominent photographic historians. A year later he moved out to the West coast to teach with the Newhalls at the California School of Fine Arts. He remained there for the next seven years, becoming friends with fellow teachers Ansel Adams and

Dorothea Lange. Together with the Newhalls, White, Adams and Lange founded the photographic magazine *Aperture*. White was made editor of the first issue and remained editor for the next twenty-three years.

During this time, White became increasingly interested in Zen philosophy and he incorporated this influence into his central theory of "Equivalence." White borrowed the term from Alfred Stieglitz, who used it to describe the use of a photograph in evoking an emotion unrelated to its subject matter. To White, the term came to stand for not only the photographer's use of the visual world as material for his expressive purposes but also as the function of relation that occurs between the object perceived and the viewer, resulting in a special sense of correspondence.

In 1965 White became head of the department of photography at the Massachusetts Institute of Technology; and in 1968 he put together the exhibition "Light 7"—the first of four highly influential exhibitions of his own and other photographers' work. These exhibitions contained, along with the photographs, lengthy quotations from him and other writers expressing his increasingly mystical approach to photography.

White's teaching remains one of his most important contributions to photography and his influence has been clearly felt and acknowledged by photographers such as Paul Caponigro.

White's only personal work combining his theories and photographs is the book *Mirrors, Messages, Manifestations,* published in 1969.

We interviewed Minor White late one evening at his house in Arlington, Massachusetts. It had snowed all day and, as we tramped up the steps onto the porch of the large wooden house, our footsteps marked a path in the perfect white cover. The door was answered by one of White's two assistants who led us into the kitchen where White was seated, finishing his supper. We introduced ourselves and his handshake seemed powerful and assured for a man almost seventy who had suffered a serious heart attack three months before. His long stern face was high-browed and his silver-white hair reached down to his shoulders. He was alert but relaxed and was dressed in a maroon Mexican serape, khaki pants, and desert boots.

We conducted the interview in a spare, gently lit room with a gas flame in the fireplace. On one wall was a Japanese brush painting and on another, a photograph of a Tantric sculpture. In the hall were several photographs by Mr. White, but in this room there were none. On the table before us was a vase of blue irises. There was a sense of dryness, simplicity, and peace in the room.

White sat in an armchair with one leg across his knee. His voice was low and controlled but never unnatural. There was always a silence between our questions and his answers in which the burning of the gas flame could be heard.

After the interview, one of his assistants showed us the basement where White had his darkroom. There was a bicycle in one corner and on the floor lay boxes of tools and old pipe sections. It looked like any other basement darkroom except for the large drying rack and the archival washer.

The sound of a Bach fugue came from the phonograph upstairs as Mr. White spent a few minutes alone before going to bed.

On June 24, 1976, four months after we interviewed him, Minor White died. He preceded the death of his friend Imogen Cunningham by several hours.

JD : I understand that you encourage your students to spend some time meditating or becoming involved with the environment before shooting.

WHITE: All the workshops, at least in the past ten years or so, have always been based on the fact that you quiet yourself down before you start to make photographs, or for that matter, to look at photographs. You just get everything else out of the way of your concentration, and you come into it as free as possible of all the things you were just thinking about. Set aside some time to let all the garbage go by so as to pay full attention to the photographing.

BC: Do you practice transcendental meditation or your own personal kind?

WHITE: The best you can say is my own personal kind.

JD: One of the books which you have all your students read is Boleslavsky's Six Lessons in Acting.

WHITE: At one time I used it very extensively for the simple reason that it was the best source available on how to approach a creative aspect of something to get ready to do it. Meditation, if you want to call it that, is involved, and this book provides the fundamental approach to something, which means you prepare yourself to do something you set out to do. You don't just tear into it. The book shows a method of *preparation* for creative work which is always effective.

JD: How did you first get interested in photography?

WHITE: My grandfather was an amateur photographer, so I was around it from crib days. I don't seem to remember his photographs, though, as much as his lantern slides, projected on the wall of a room set aside for slide shows.

JD: Do you remember when you got your first camera?

WHITE: I'm under the impression that I got a little one, a Box Brownie, and then somehow later I got a little bigger one. I suspect it was on a birthday. Seventh, eighth, ninth . . . I don't recall.

17

JD : So you don't remember your first photograph?

WHITE: I've got a couple around the house. Maybe not the first one, but around that time. A photograph of my best friend, and my grandmother, and a squash.

JD : As far as expressing yourself artistically though, I understand your first love was poetry.

WHITE: During high school, I was photographing and I was doing a little writing. The amount of writing was minute . . . the amount of photographing was minute! But they were going on simultaneously. As far as any aesthetic aspects go, at that date I had some dim notion about aesthetics—not under those terms, of course. My grandfather had his house contracting office in an art gallery and I used to visit him on Saturday a great deal, and was exposed to all kinds of art in a very good commercial gallery, the top gallery in Minneapolis. At that time, of course, the art shown was pretty romantic gooey stuff, and I loved it.

I was trying to write poetry. I knew that poetry was something a little more special than prose. And I was photographing landscapes primarily, similar to the foggy landscapes I saw at the art gallery. I used to go to Minnehaha Creek to photograph trees in fog leaning over the water, or the water with spots of foam floating under the bridge. I was reading Japanese poems at the time.

JD : You were drafted in 1942, and then were baptized into the Catholic church a year later. Is there any correlation between the two?

WHITE: Some. I was going with a girlfriend who was Catholic, and she went into the WACs the same time as I was drafted into the army. We spent a weekend together talking about the prospect of being in the war, and she thought that I might just as well join the Catholic church—"it can't do you any harm, and it might do you some good." You see, I'd take her to church, and then I'd go out photographing while I was waiting. As far as I could tell, we were both doing the same thing. She couldn't perceive it that way, but that didn't change my habits. I went right on photographing while she went to mass. But after getting in the army and not being allowed to photograph, I had more time to pray. I had plenty of time to study so I approached the chaplain, and in a relatively short time, he baptized me into the Catholic church.

JD : The way you tell it, it doesn't sound as if it was of any profound significance.

WHITE: I have given the wrong impression unintentionally.

JD : Were you always inclined towards religion of some kind?

WHITE: Yes. I started searching for a place to go to church when I was about fifteen. The morning services always bored the hell out of me, but the evening services would often be interesting, so I shopped around evening services of various churches. I also read a good deal of material on living with nature. These authors who had profound religious experiences with their outdoor life fitted me very well. I could go along with that because they weren't preaching religion. They were direct, and that corresponded with my experiences in nature.

JD : Your view of nature is quite similar to Wordsworth's.

WHITE: Yes. I can't say which came first, whether I was already inclined that way, or whether the nature poets inclined me that way, but I found that I leaned toward writers who wrote emotionally about the spiritual manifestations and the esoteric manifestations in the great outdoors. William Blake became a very great favorite while I was in college.

JD : And your religious inclinations today?

WHITE: They're much the same. What I was trying to learn with Catholicism was how this particular religion functioned, and its custom. Learning about it in a war theater at the time, the rituals were pared down to essentials. The chaplain would find a stump somewhere and lay a couple of things on it, and the first thing you knew, he had his altar. In that area, I could function with it. But I remember when I got home, I went to a Catholic church, and there was a whole array of this stuff, and I kind of wondered what happened to what's supposed to go on here. I couldn't make contact with the essence of it. So I just stopped going.

BC : Were you in combat in the army?

WHITE: I was in a combat unit although I was not at any point actually shooting at anybody; but not too many yards away, my friends were.

BC : Did you keep a journal?

WHITE: Mostly a series of aphorisms and long poems. The much edited result of the journal is the sequence "Amputations," in the book *Mirrors, Messages, Manifestations*. That was the culmination of all the writing that was done during service. The portraits in the sequence were made in the army too, in the Hawaiian Islands. The rest of the pix were done after the war at Point Lobos, California.

An exhibition of about fifty of these portraits with poems under them was planned, but never materialized. When I finally edited the pictures and poems for a second show, it was trimmed unmercifully to what is published in *Mirrors, Messages, Manifestations*.

JD : So you have been pretty much a free spirit since you left the army.

WHITE: I may attempt to be a free spirit without causing too much of an uproar on the immediate surroundings.

JD : Is the lifestyle of an artist very important to you?

WHITE: Well, my lifestyle—I don't know if I'm an artist or not—my lifestyle is mighty important to me.

BC : How were you able to support yourself during the early years?

WHITE: When I started to do photography seriously, after I moved from Minneapolis to Portland, Oregon in 1937, I said, "all right, from here on, I'm going to be a photographer." I had no money, no camera, nothing—but I got going. I had been writing verse for a good five years very seriously, and I had somewhere along the line realized that there was a certain feeling state that occurred when I was writing poetry well; I would have a certain feeling state saying "Well, something's finished," and I came to the conclusion about that time that "now I know what it is to be 'creative.'" I kind of shudder when I use the word "creative" now, but not then, forty years ago.

Anyway, I had deliberately set up a five-year-plan to write verse and see whether I could make any money. I failed completely. So I returned to an earlier love, the camera. I said, "I know what's central to any creative work and all I have to do now is to learn the rudiments of photography—the essential inner state I already know." I don't know how I knew all that, but I talked to myself in those words. So I gave myself a five-year-plan for photography, and in two and a half years or less, I was having one-man shows that later traveled, and I made a name for myself in Portland in that short a time because I knew what it was I was after.

JD : So this was before you'd worked with people like Dorothea Lange and Ansel Adams?

WHITE: Yes, this was long before. I went from the Portland area into the army, and after the army I was in New York studying art history and photo history for a year. That's when I began to personally meet well-known photographers for the first time. In 1946 I went to San Francisco and started to teach photography formally at the then-named California School of Fine Arts.

JD : How did you teach yourself photography?

WHITE: I read all the books on photography available at the Portland Public Library. I had learned the rudiments of processing in college. Someone just showed me how and that's the way I did it. So I learned very much on my own, with the help of books and friends in the Portland Camera Club. In college I'd been working in chemistry labs and I'd gotten some notion of how laboratory functions worked and I just used that to learn photography.

JD : Did the science of photography appeal to you as much as the art?

WHITE: No. The science of it has never been very interesting to me.

BC : Did you have any problems seeing where you were going as a young photographer?

WHITE: It did not seem to bother me. To be sure there were problems, and correct exposure was the most difficult. I belonged to the Camera Club in Oregon where exposure and aesthetics were discussed at *great* length and heatedly. The same problem would come up week after week, and year after year, till pretty soon I got to know all those problems and deal with them.

JD : Can we move on to when you were in California with Ansel Adams?

WHITE: Ansel had started his course in photography at the California Institute of Fine Arts in May, 1946; I landed there in July and I started teaching immediately. Ansel Adams gave a lecture one morning on the Zone System and I was out in the afternoon helping kids trying to do it. I think they probably knew more about it than I did; but some of them knew less, so I talked to those.

BC : Was hearing about the Zone System something special?

WHITE: It was fantastic listening to Ansel that morning. There was nothing published on it at that time and I'd heard nothing about it, and sitting up in class, my problems with exposure cleared up, pronto! All my struggles in Portland to try to figure out how the relationship between exposure and development and so on which I had been working at, but not getting anywhere, just fell into place. From there on, the only troubles were with execution. The theory was crystalline clear.

BC : Was this the same sort of feeling you had when reading about equivalence?

WHITE: No. Equivalence was learned bit by bit over twenty

years. I had encountered it when I was still in Portland through the books of Alfred Stieglitz, and I was very much involved in it. I read that part very carefully, but only six years later in San Francisco did I start to photograph equivalents.

The idea got to me very slowly. It took me a long time to grasp what it meant, but when I started doing it, it was familiar enough that it was not difficult. There were no great shocks and excitements about it.

JD : Which other photographers did you like at that time?

WHITE: Weston and Adams. I was reading the current photo magazines as well as books, and I met their work through the magazines.

JD : When was the first time you felt ready to write about photography and your own feelings about photography?

WHITE: I started writing an article called "When is photography creative?" which was published a few months after I wrote it in *American Photography*. This was about 1941. It was a pretty naïve little article.

JD : What about the founding of Aperture?

WHITE: There had been a conference of photographers at Aspen with some fifty photographers there for a week doing nothing but talking photographs to each other and giving conferences and lectures, listening to concerts and so on—one of those very concentrated things—and one afternoon, there was a discussion of a possible publication for serious photography. There was a going magazine by the Photographic Society of America and there was lots of discussion about why not just infiltrate and make this thing into the kind of magazine we wanted, or why not just start a whole brand new one. Nothing was concluded that afternoon, obviously, but a few months later, Nancy Newhall and Ansel and myself and a couple of other people were sitting around Ansel's fireplace drinking martinis, and a discussion got going on photographic magazines, and Ansel pulled out a little sheet that he and Beaumont and Nancy had put together a couple of years before. They'd called it "Light," and the same kind of discussion came up, but we got a few more

23

people together with a lawyer and decided, well, let's do it. So Ansel wrote 25 letters asking for $25 a piece in order to get it off the ground, and he got 25 letters back; only one of them had $12.50 instead of $25.00 and an explanation. That's what *Aperture* started on.

The position of editor just fell to me by accident. I didn't want it, but Ansel was too busy, Dorothy Lange was too rushed, somebody else was too this, somebody else was too that, and by the time it got to me, I said, "Well, I'm just too out of it" and so they said, "All right, you're the editor."

JD : How did you come up with the name Aperture?

WHITE: As always, that was a long struggle, full of laughs and senseless fantasizing.

JD : Do you enjoy magazines as a showplace?

WHITE: Of course. I also like putting them together. I found that when the first issue [of *Aperture*] was finally published, I was all ready to do another one; and another, and another, for about fifteen years.

JD : Are you concerned by the difference between a photograph being seen in a magazine or on a wall?

WHITE: A book gives you the intimacy of the images, the wall gives you the grandeur of the stuff, and you can't usually get both at the same time.

BC : Do you take color photographs?

WHITE: Hundreds of them, thousands of them. But always color transparencies, no prints. I use my color slides mainly for lectures and classroom use. They get a lot more use than most of my black-and-whites, but not as much public exposure.

JD : What do you like about color transparencies?

WHITE: The color. I like the color, and the lovely sense of light, and the fact that large on a wall they affect people rapidly and effectively.

BC : *Do you ever print these transparencies as photographs?*

WHITE: Rarely—I'm not sure why. Maybe because I don't have to be in the darkroom at all, it's just an editing process. I send it out to the local drugstore, the best Kodak processing. I tried the custom processors and they came out worse.

BC : *Do you ever shoot the same subject in color and black-and-white in the same day?*

WHITE: The same minute. Shoot both cameras at once.

JD : *What kind of cameras do you use?*

WHITE: I use 35mm, $2\frac{1}{4}$x$3\frac{1}{4}$, and 4x5. I like the camera in my hand better than all the others.

JD : *Do you play around much with the negative in the darkroom?*

WHITE: If I have the time I do. In the last four or five years, I've done much more with sandwiched negatives, double exposures, solarization, and reversals.

JD : *Could you discuss what goes on in the case of one particular photograph, how the final image is arrived at? One that comes to mind is from the* Jupiter *portfolio—an interior of a room with a curtain blowing slightly in front of an open window and there is a swirl of glowing light just underneath it on the wall. Could you tell how you came to take this picture?*

WHITE: It was very simple. I was sitting at breakfast one day and the light was coming across my shoulder from behind me and it hit some wire chairs behind which was some glass; the sunlight bounced off the glass onto the wall where you see it in the photograph. It was just straight, something I saw. All I had to do was set the camera up and photograph it—no manipulation whatsoever.

JD : *Are you ever surprised by what you see, despite previsualization?*

WHITE: Once in a while I'll say "What idiot did that? I couldn't have done it." But it's on my roll of film.

25

JD : But you're also sometimes surprised in a good way.

WHITE: I accept it as a gift of the gods if I like it and throw it away if I don't.

I have had the experience of being in the darkroom and printing a negative from the West coast that had never excited me, then getting it up 11x14 and just have the top of my head go right off. At the time I took it I didn't see it that way, and then, *whammo!* And that still happens periodically. I "explain" this phenomenon as while photographing, the "technician" takes over and obscures the emotional side from my view. When printing, the emotional side takes over.

BC : Do you ever have a hard time accepting pictures as your own that came out differently than the way you previsualized them? Do you feel uncomfortable claiming them as your own work, the result of your own vision?

WHITE: When gifts are given to me through my camera I accept them graciously.

BC : I think you once said that you have to have the picture come to accept you in such a case. That you had to live with the image for a while before you could claim it.

WHITE: Quite true. Sometimes we work so fast that we don't really understand what's going on in front of the camera. We just kind of sense that "Oh my God, it's significant!" and photograph impulsively while trying to get the exposure right. Exposure occupies my mind while intuition frames the image.

BC : Do you have a decisive moment, or is it more a period of decision coming to grips with the importance of a longer moment?

WHITE: Very often in photographing, intellectually I know instantly that the photograph is there. Sometimes emotionally I feel it very powerfully. Other times I don't feel it at all. But I expose anyway, trusting something in me.

Often the area where I am photographing is not conducive to meditation, so I don't do it. I may have other things to consider besides meditating when I'm in the middle of a highway. But the danger intensifies seeing almost as if I were meditating.

BC: *What is it about nature that has attracted you so much?*

WHITE: I like to get my feet wet in creeks and fall down in lakes, play in the snow and mud, build rock dams, and I have always enjoyed that.

BC: *Are you trying to express any larger themes in your photographs? To communicate your feelings as one man in nature or as an expression of all men in nature?*

WHITE: I don't think it's all that complicated. Sometimes I find myself getting in tune with it, and photographing when I am in tune feels great! And I want to share my feelings. I have often photographed when I was not in tune with nature but the photographs look as if I had been. So I conclude that something in nature says "come and take my photograph." So I do, regardless of how I feel.

I don't usually conceptualize while photographing. I'm not worried about the relationship of man to nature. If I'm making equivalents of that relationship, I find it out later.

JD: *As far as the creative process is concerned, is it what you were saying before, that nature calls you to take its picture?*

WHITE: The creative process is quite a topic. I've been writing about this for many years and some day I'm going to write it the way I think it's correct. It will probably come down to four words: "elephants live on lilypads." People will wonder what the hell I am talking about, but that's a common experience among people who attempt to define creativity from a heart experience of it.

Just recently I had it all set out. I was kind of half-dreaming and I finally got it all down that God and creativity are together. I wrote it many times, finally I got it right, properly spaced on the page and everything else. I came back to it the next day and it made no sense at all. This didn't surprise me because it's happened so often before. It is a great effort to get it down this way. At the time it seems to evolve into what you're trying to get down; afterwards, you're in a different frame of mind and it doesn't fit any more. But at the moment it is connected. One is in a very strange state oftentimes, one which we're not normally in, and the words used in that state don't fit the words in our ordinary state.

JD: What about the Freudian interpretation of the creative process: that artists produce work to gain fame, money, and sexual love?

WHITE: That's probably the same thing as what I just said. That in the right frame of mind it means something, but in the other frame of mind it's just garbage. The Freudian interpretation only covers the ordinary life state. It omits other states, and even denies their existence.

JD: What do you think of the work of Frederick Sommer?

WHITE: One of my favorite photographers. He's been a friend of mine for a long time. We have a great deal in common.

JD: Did you do the editing on his Aperture *monograph?*

WHITE: All I did was just pry. One summer I went out to Arizona, where he lives, and talked to him for a week or so about doing a book, and I said, "Next time I come out here, I want to see a book laid out!" His wife explained to me later that only the night before I came did he lay it out.

JD: The exhibits you put together have been mostly other people's work.

WHITE: I always stick one of my own in for the fun of it. But I selected to a theme in my head—so far as I could—with the photographs kindly submitted to me for editing.

BC: What do you think of the work that's being done by younger photographers? Do you find any trends that you are interested in, or puzzled by, or critical of?

WHITE: All three categories that you mention and more. I think it's very exciting that people visually try everything they can. There's no particular class of photograph that I think is any better than any other class. I'm always and forever looking for the image that has spirit! I don't give a damn how it got made.

BC: Are there photographers working now who you feel receive unearned praise?

28

WHITE: Of course. The trash that gets up as art in art and photography galleries would make a person regurgitate his favorite steak dinner. But amidst the garbage are the gems. I look for those and worry not about the rest.

JD : There seems to be a constant striving for originality in the new photography. Young photographers have a dilemma which comes from the fact that they can take a photograph which would be very much like a Weston, or an Evans, or a Minor White, and they could be completely unaware of your work or someone else's, and yet their work will be branded, or at least seen, as derivative. Do you see any solution to that?

WHITE: The obvious solution is to eliminate the phony criticism that abounds today. Another solution is to look into any young photographer, then ask: are any of his pictures as good as or better than Edward Weston, Walker Evans, or whoever. The material is out there for anyone to use. Everything in the world has been photographed a few million times and it does not stop.

At this time in the history of photography, everything has been done. All the novelties have been done; yet the pseudo-critics ask for more pseudo-originality. All we have to look for now is, as a picture, does it move my heartstrings? If it does, why should I condemn it just because it happens to look like something Weston did?

Few young people have the power, but every once in a while, one does come through with as much power as Weston had. It is the nourishment value of the image that matters. Whether it looks like another photographer's work is a side issue, swollen out of all proportion today.

BC : In other words, young photographers should not feel trapped or channeled into following a course of art history.

WHITE: There's no point to throwing that road to discovery away either. The point is to make a photograph which has the power of the original subject!

A lot of times, imitations are weak imitations. Look at Strand's work and Weston's work and you'll see that they photographed a lot of the same subject matter, but they both come up with power. Photographers who come up with power never get accused of imitating anyone else, even though they photograph the same broom, same street, same portraits.

JD : In viewing a photograph, is anything more than a degree of self-awareness needed in order to come away from it with a meaningful reading? Is a knowledge of the technical limitations necessary?

WHITE: The more knowledge (including the technical, psychological, historical, and personal) that a viewer brings to a photograph, the richer will be his experience. He will be able to see it on many levels and hopefully without having to criticize it on any level. What usually destroys the experience of a photograph is to start criticizing it. Criticism has its rightful place in the whole experiencing of photographs and photographing. Let's keep it there.

JD : One of my favorite statements of yours is : "To think of photography as some degree of glorified Rorschach test is not detrimental to either medium."

WHITE: I was aiming that one at Ansel. And he reacted!

JD : What about titling your work?

WHITE: They have to have titles for filing purposes when they're published or in a museum.

JD : What about choice of titles?

WHITE: That becomes quite a lark in itself. Edward Weston would just put an absolutely nondescript title on his works and that seemed to satisfy people's urge to have something written down in the corner. But a poet can write a few words under it which will change how you see it. In this case words and picture will affect each other, they enlarge each other.

JD : To you, the object photographed is not as important as the mental image that the viewer carries away, is it?

WHITE: They are equally important to me. The photo acts as a continual source of audience response for me. As more people tell me about their experience with a given image, it grows in magnitude for me.

*JD : In very few of your photographs is there a deliberate juxta-position of images to create the movement, but there are one or two—*Two Barns and Shadow, *for instance, taken with infrared film. Can you say why you used that film at the time?*

WHITE: I had been using a lot of infrared film that fall, and I knew that the scene was flat. I made a normal picture of it too. The infrared exaggerated, but not beyond, my feeling about it. I was very moved by the scene, so I highly overdramatized it through the infrared. In the darkroom I was very excited, and it is still one I return to often with pleasure.

JD : What goes through your mind at the moment you release the shutter?

WHITE: A large vacuum filled with anticipation.

JD : Do you find that you lose your awareness of the camera at that moment?

WHITE: Certainly not. The click of the shutter is part of the camera. I'm very aware of the camera.

JD : What do you think of the Polaroids, the SX-70 for example?

WHITE: I think they are great. They change everything. It's this fast business, seeing it right away, that is exciting to anybody. That is its major value. There's nothing spectacular about the photographs themselves beyond normal expectations.

BC : Have you ever used a movie camera?

WHITE: No. I don't have enough time. If I ever make a movie, I want to do it well, not just dabble. Life is too short.

BC : As a photographer, do you find that you see photographically all the time, or do you turn it off and on when you're shooting with a camera?

WHITE: I'm always mentally photographing everything as practice.

31

JD : Do you ever go out to photograph with a specific purpose in mind? You have a certain feeling you want to express and you go out to find an image that will satisfy this?

WHITE: Yes, very often I deliberately try to find something that matches a feeling I have. On the other hand, a lot of times I photograph with nothing specific in mind. I just play it as it comes. If it's good, fine. I find "letting it happen" relaxing, a playful vacation. Stimulating pictures almost always result.

BC : In your book, Mirrors, Messages, Manifestations *you refer to "Camera," capital C, no article before it, and to "Darkroom." Could you explain this?*

WHITE: Well, that simply means the practice of Camera, the idea of Camera, which of course grows out of cameras. It's a generalization. Sometimes you find yourself speaking of Camera, not having any particular camera in mind at all, but just the action that one does go through in using a camera— and also the results, the photographs themselves and their relationship to people. It's an abstraction which includes a lot.

BC : Do you feel that creative power makes you a receptor for something special?

WHITE: No more than you or anybody else. This is not something that happens to just some people, it's the birthright of all of us. I think that everyone without exception has similar experiences now and then, and because they don't happen often enough, they don't follow through. It happens to them once in a while, and then it happens less and less *unless* they follow it up, unless they say "My gosh, where did that come from?" and start to search for where it came from and deliberately try to have more such experiences. If they don't do that, then these flashes get less and less and less and less and finally cease.

But as young people, the first "visions" are given to us to let us know that they are possible, otherwise we wouldn't know that. These things that blow my mind and are very exciting and all that, if they hadn't happened, I would never have known it could happen. But knowing that it can, I make efforts to try and repeat it. I go in search instead of just waiting till it happens. I seek out places where it can happen more readily, such as deserts, or mountains, or solitary areas, or by myself with a seashell, and when I'm there get into states of mind where I'm more open than usual. I'm waiting, I'm listening. I go to those places and make myself ready through meditation. Through being quiet and willing to wait, I can begin to see the inner man and the essence of the subject in front of me. I reach for the esoteric side of my life and usually nature cooperates. So do man-made artifacts—so do people. . . . Watching the way the current moves a blade of grass—sometimes I've seen that happen and it has just turned me inside out.

BC : What about doing that artificially with drugs?

WHITE: The basic trouble there is that the people who use the drugs do not do it in connection with meditation, and in order to do the job, there needs to be hours and hours of preparation to put yourself into a place and into a frame of mind where this drug can have its effect in the right way. Later there needs to be a withdrawal, also done in a ceremonial way so that it's done right. Then, these experiences can be very beneficial on many counts; otherwise they tend to be harmful. Usually beginners abuse drugs. They need guidance to use drugs to their advantage. Nothing short of prayer will lead to proper use. Indians have known this for centuries.

JD : How do you see social photography? Do you think it has an effect on people's sensibilities?

WHITE: It most obviously does affect people. It brutalizes people who would otherwise be less brutal; because it doesn't touch them, they're not being hurt themselves. We throw millions and millions of pictures at people without considering their effect.

But pictures can also be healing. Working with classes, studying photographs at great length, spending half an hour to an hour on a specific photograph, some get the sensation that they have been met in a place in themselves where they don't want to be, yet they faced it. I've seen people digest an experience which has no bearing on the photograph under scrutiny. For example, after half an hour of looking at one of my photographs, a student turned to me and said, "Now I know what love is." I don't know whether that was a situation of healing, but it

33

certainly brought about a moment of understanding something. There are photographs I've lived by for years on end.

JD : There has been a lot of quite hostile criticism to your exhibitions. In particular, there was Alan Hudson's criticism of Celebration *which seemed to me to revolve around the suitability of prayer as a theme and your approach to it rather than the actual photographs. Were you surprised by this?*

WHITE: I was a little surprised by the violence with which he went at it. That upset me for a couple of days. As to whether prayer is suitable for exhibition—Good Lord, we go to museums and see religious art constantly.

JD : We haven't talked much about sequencing. Can you say something about that?

WHITE: Well, it always seemed to me the logical thing to do with a bunch of photographs—give them an order so that the person who's looking at them is, if he chooses to follow that order, seeing them in a sequence which I feel will affect him in a certain way. I may be all wrong, but if he does that, then he sees it, he hears my sentence in the order which I say it to him.

By using the sequential form, while I can't control anybody to see them in that order, it just allows the person who takes the time to wonder why I've put them in that order and perhaps see what was said. Photographs side by side cannot help being mutually affected. Transpose them, the meaning changes. Sequencing is a means of trying to channel the way in which a series of pictures is seen for the sake of the meaning that comes out in that order.

BC : You rarely use one subject in which the subject itself changes over the sequence.

WHITE: I do tend to use different subject matter from photograph to photograph rather than taking a pumpkin and turning it around a few times, but it's probably a built-in personal preference with no more significance than that.

BC : Is there any sense of time you would like the viewer to come away with?

34

WHITE: A sense of time is of the least interest to me. I don't care whether one thinks it all happened in a flash or over ten thousand years. What happened is what interests me. What went on. What experience one has.

JD : Is there one of your sequences you like best?

WHITE: One called "These Images" is my favorite, I think, and I made it a very long time ago.

JD : Could you comment on some of your contemporaries in photography?

WHITE: I'd rather not. All of them are doing what they need to be doing and it's very exciting to hear how they rationalize their seeing—just like I do. Whether I agree or disagree, it's amazing what people say they want to do.

BC : What about formalist issues in pictures?

WHITE: That's a part of picture-taking again, but if we get too wrapped up in formalism, you forget to make pictures. Any photograph has a certain formal aspect and the idea of carrying it to the point where you just extract the form and let everything else go gives you a pretty sterile photograph, just as subject matter to the exclusion of formal considerations tends to be commonplace.

JD : Thank you very much, Mr. White. Before we finish, do you have anything you would like to add?

WHITE: It seems to me that the important thing has been said, namely, any form that photography happens to take can be transcended.
    A Zen saying: when someone's pointing at the moon, why look at his thumb?

Imogen Cunningham

Imogen Cunningham was born in Portland, Oregon, in 1883. She studied chemistry at the University of Washington and after graduation took a job at the Curtis Studio in Seattle, printing Edward S. Curtis's Indian pictures on platinum paper. In 1910 she opened a portrait studio in Seattle, at which time her work, heavily influenced by Gertrude Kasebier, consisted of romantic soft-focus pictures, often symbolically or narratively conceived.

She married in 1915 and, restricted by the responsibilities of marriage, her photography became directed towards the plant forms around her house. She later divorced her husband and returned to portraiture and nudes.

In 1932 Cunningham became one of the original members of Group ƒ64. This group, highly influential in American photography, was founded by Willard Van Dyke and Ansel Adams, and included Edward Weston. Their aim was to promote simple and straightforward technique and to this end used a large view camera, and employed the smallest focal apertures—ƒ64 being the smallest—to achieve finely detailed images. They usually made their prints on smooth paper, and gave great attention to achieving a maximum range of tones from black to white.

In the fifties and sixties, Cunningham's photography ranged

from street work to portraits of movie stars, and she taught at the San Francisco Art Institute. Her last work included a study of old age.

A year before her death, Imogen Cunningham created a trust to supervise the distribution and exhibition of her photographs. The trust releases unsigned prints that have been stamped with the mark of the Chinese "chop" which Cunningham specifically requested for her signature. The mark consists of three Chinese characters which represent phonetically the name "Imogen" (Im o gen). The translation of the characters is fitting: "Ideas without end."

I interviewed Imogen Cunningham in her small cottage-style house on Russian Hill in San Francisco where she has lived alone for almost thirty years. It was a spring day and her garden was filled with succulents and other plants, many of which she had photographed over the years. Inside the house, the small living room was casual and run-down. No one was in the room. There were no photographs or paintings on the walls, but in one corner stood a draped store mannequin.

"Just a minute," said a voice and I turned to see Cunningham shuffle into the room. She was white-haired and tiny, barely five feet tall, and seemed a cross between a pioneer woman and a fairy

37

godmother. She took me in with a critical glance and sat herself down in a chair. "Which one are you?" she said, "and why did I let you in?" I identified myself and then asked the purpose of the mannequin. "Oh her," said Cunningham, adjusting her glasses. "She's just a friend. Don't pay any attention to her."

The interview lasted two hours. At about halfway, Cunningham stopped to look out the window at a cat which was stalking a bird. "Yours?" I asked. "Definitely not," she replied tersely. "I'm not an animal herder." Her voice had the tremor of age in it and she faltered on some syllables, but her mind was clear and the time passed quickly.

Near the end of the interview she said to me, "I hope you're the last person who interviews me." As it turned out, I was. Two months later Imogen Cunningham went into the hospital and died peacefully on June 24, 1976. She was ninety-three.

IMOGEN CUNNINGHAM: What are you going to do with this trash?

BC : It will be included in a book of interviews.

CUNNINGHAM: That's not a good enough reason. I'm not so curious about everybody's life. I like biography myself, but I don't like little snips of questions and answers. I like somebody who really knows what he's writing about. Now the other day a man came to interview me about Dorothea Lange. That's the way to do it—wait until I'm dead, then get the real truth from someone who knew me.

You know this business of asking questions like "Did you have difficulty getting your first job?" Well, in answer to that: I didn't. I learned platinum printing and got a job working for Edward S. Curtis.

BC : Were you interested in Indians or was it just the offer of the job?

CUNNINGHAM: Both. I grew up with something of the Indians around me and I learned very quickly that nobody treated them right. When I saw Curtis's work in 1909, I knew he was a great photographer. He was tremendously motivated by what he thought might save the Indian race. Many people misjudge him now by saying he dressed his subjects up to look like what they had been. That was true in some cases, but most looked like that.

BC : Did he believe that his photography could change things?

CUNNINGHAM: He had expected a more rightful attitude towards the Indian, naturally. He was an ambitious man, no doubt about that, and completely devoted to them.

BC : Do you remember your first photograph?

CUNNINGHAM: No, I don't. But I bought my first camera in 1901 from an international correspondence school in Pennsylvania. It cost me fifteen dollars for the camera, some glass-plates and a box to send them back and forth in. And a book of directions. When I had learned all I could about developing and printing from this gadget, I sold it to another gal and taught her. There were no photographers in Seattle at that time except commercial ones and I didn't like them. I had seen something I did like though and that was the work of Gertrude Kasebier. Her work was published in a magazine called *The Craftsman.*

BC : Did you try to imitate her?

CUNNINGHAM: No, I just said to myself, "There is a photographer. Why haven't I seen anything this good before?"

BC : Did you have what you would call a "normal" childhood?

CUNNINGHAM: I was a backward child in many ways. I didn't enter school until I was eight years old but I thought it was marvelous to learn to read. I promptly read Dante's *Inferno* and didn't understand it. My mother was practically illiterate but my father read a great deal and would talk to me about books.

I came from a big family but I didn't get much attention or encouragement for my photography. I was a loner as far as that was concerned. I didn't pay any attention to anyone else, I just wanted to learn.

BC : What about your own parents' influence on you?

CUNNINGHAM: My father was not interested in photography. He said to me, "Why do you want to go to school for so long if all you turn out to be is a dirty photographer?" He had seen them all with their dripping aprons and wanted me to be a nice schoolteacher instead. But he never mentioned it after that and built a darkroom in the woodshed for me. He never praised me. I took a picture of him when he was ninety that sells almost more than any other I've made. He took a correspondence course in mathematics at the age of sixty-seven and was interested in the work of Ouspensky. He believed in reincarnation and was a theosophist. I attended many lectures with him on that subject.

I was always interested in art. In grammar school the teacher put me on the left-hand side of the class so that I could draw all the students after I had finished my studies. My father thought I had a gift and sent me to a private art school on Saturdays and during the summer.

BC: So was most of your visual training from painting?

CUNNINGHAM: Yes. Very little from photography. I used to buy Perry pictures which were reproductions of paintings. I remember seeing the original in Boston of a painting and having been very deluded about the size from the Perry picture. But there weren't very many photographs reproduced in magazines in those days, so there was very little communication.

BC: I understand that when you left Seattle in 1917 you destroyed a great number of photographic plates. Why?

CUNNINGHAM: I did it because they were too heavy and bulky to carry.

BC: You have no regrets about having to do that?

CUNNINGHAM: Well, what's the use of crying over spilled milk? Everybody has some disaster in his life. There was one image, however, that I regret not being able to keep. It was of a young blond boy nude on a Persian rug.

BC: What made you give up your early romantic style of photography?

CUNNINGHAM: I don't know whether I did.

BC: *What were some of the influences on your work?*

CUNNINGHAM: My greatest influence for portraiture was Utamaro, the Japanese print-maker.

BC: *Can you explain?*

CUNNINGHAM: It's not easy to pose people together. They either repel each other or don't seem sympathetic with each other. Utamaro did it splendidly. I used one of his compositions to photograph two people together to illustrate a poem, a man and woman nude in the woods.

BC: *Are you interested in the philosophical theories that other photographers have created? Like Wynn Bullock's Fourth Dimension?*

CUNNINGHAM: I never read the junk.

BC: *Do you have a personal philosophy about photography?*

CUNNINGHAM: No, I do not. I have some ideas, but I won't call it a philosophy. I'm not a philosopher.

BC: *Does the idea of equivalence interest you?*

CUNNINGHAM: That's all bunk. I don't work on anyone's formula and I think that was a formula.

BC: *What do you feel at the moment you press the shutter release?*

CUNNINGHAM: Couldn't possibly imagine.

BC: *Is it a blank?*

CUNNINGHAM: No, I always think, "I've got it!" I don't punch it until I know I've got it, but even then I don't always get it.

BC: *Cartier-Bresson's decisive moment?*

CUNNINGHAM: He was sure right. Once a woman who does street work said to me, "I've never photographed anyone I haven't asked first." I said to her, "Suppose Cartier-Bresson asked the man who jumped the puddle to do it again—it never would have been the same. Start stealing!"

BC: Were you familiar with the photographer Alvin Langdon Coburn?

CUNNINGHAM: I saw him several times in London when I made my first trip to Europe in 1909. He was a very intelligent person in spite of the fact that he had a very domineering mother. She was what I would call something of a horror. When Alvin went out of the room to get a book, she said to me, "You could never be as good a photographer as Alvin." I replied, "Well, I hadn't thought of trying."

BC: He suggested in 1916 something that I think applies to the work you and Edward Weston and others did later: "that there should be an exhibit of abstract photographs in which the interest of the subject matter would be secondary to the appreciation of the extraordinary."

CUNNINGHAM: Well, he said a lot of things. Sometime after that he went off to his old home and absolutely buried himself in some occult beliefs. He was that way for a long time.

BC: I'd like to ask you . . .

CUNNINGHAM: If you don't ask me about my love life, I will like you. I think that's nobody's business, don't you agree? I was interviewed recently and this woman asked if I had any affairs before I was married and I said, "Who cares?" She wanted to make a big story like Edward Weston's. That was her idea of an interesting story. I think that if there's anything interesting about a photographer then it must be what he does, not his private life. Certainly Edward Weston's life spoiled him for me. I think he was disreputable. It doesn't matter how many times a person is married, it's the way he cast them off that bothers me. He would get a new woman and then go back to the one he cast off.

BC: What did you think of Stieglitz's work?

CUNNINGHAM: Everybody likes Stieglitz's work. His work would be a credit to anyone who could do it. He didn't do such a tremendous amount, but he didn't make as many mistakes as a lot of other photographers did.

BC: What mistakes did other photographers make that he didn't?

CUNNINGHAM: I think Edward Weston made plenty of mistakes. He printed a lot of rotten prints and signed his name to them. Stieglitz never did that.

BC: Could you talk about your relationship with Stieglitz?

CUNNINGHAM: I went to his gallery 291 on my way back from Germany. He was the first person brave enough to try to have photographs for sale in a gallery. He started *Camera Work* in 1902 and the gallery in 1905. He was a frightfully dictatorial person. The Photo-Secession was all his idea; and it excluded certain kinds of people.

BC: What kind of people did he mean to exclude?

CUNNINGHAM: The millions of so-called "commercial photographers." In San Francisco I call them "Market Street photographers"—the kind that blow things up and retouch all the reality out of the print.

BC: Whom did he mean to include then?

CUNNINGHAM: He included photographers who seceded from banality and formulas.

BC: What do you consider to be the value of Camera Work?

CUNNINGHAM: I think it is the most important contribution to the reproduction of photography that has ever been done. It set a standard. It fascinated me and I studied it avidly.

BC: Did Stieglitz ever exhibit any of your work?

CUNNINGHAM: No. The only Western photographer that I know he was interested in was Ann Brigman. She was almost exclusively interested in the nude. She was the wife of a sea captain and she had gone on one trip to sea with him and had fallen into the hold of the ship. The result was that she had to have an operation and have one breast removed. That was a great handicap because she was her own model. She always used to get herself up in a pitchy tree and set the camera below. Then she would try to conceal that one breast, make the photograph, and call it "The Dryad." Then she would retouch anything that was necessary. When I look back on what she did and what Stieglitz picked out, I feel that his judgment at that time was just as faulty as anyone else's. After the Secession, an organization called the Pictorialists appeared and I joined them.

BC: *What about Steichen?*

CUNNINGHAM: He was a great commercial man. After he became head of that special group of officers in the Navy during the Second World War, he got very large in the head. He really loved himself tremendously. He made a great blow about anyone who joined him—a great honor, you know. Then he went on to do the *Family of Man* show.

BC: *Did you have any work in that show?*

CUNNINGHAM: No, I was turned down. It wasn't the kind of exhibition that photographers themselves get very much out of. It was an exhibition of people for people. The theme was interesting, but the exhibit was designed for the Museum of Modern Art specifically and it often wasn't exhibited with adequate space in other places. The way the show was laid out in San Francisco, you came around the corner and you were immediately face-to-face with something ten feet high and eight feet wide. You couldn't get away from those big, out-of-focus photographic blobs.

BC: *Did the* Family of Man *show arouse interest in photography as well as in* Man?

CUNNINGHAM: I think people looked at that show just as they would a copy of *Life* magazine. That's all right, but most people just think of photographs as something that is simply a way to present subject matter, not as an art form with all its complexity. My son Rondal had something in that show.

BC: I haven't seen any of your son's work.

CUNNINGHAM: Nobody ever has. He doesn't care for show or honors, he just wants to earn a living. In the War he was in submarines, photographing the men in action. After that with Time-Life and another big publisher in the East. The other day I asked him what he was doing and he said, "Oh, I'm selling art," and I asked, "What's that?" He replied, "Something nobody needs." He's selling to a decorator. He combines photographs in decorative shapes and makes prints on aluminium that are eighteen feet long and eight feet wide, and that's a decoration for a dark restaurant. All restaurants are dark.

BC: Do you think photojournalism has helped audiences accept other forms of photography simply by the great exposure provided by the magazines? Has it helped make photography an art form distinct from painting and more than just a snapshot?

CUNNINGHAM: I don't know if it gave people a better estimate of photography or not. It is a different kind of photography and I think people should divide photography into its different phases and be aware that there are differences.

BC: Do you feel, as Ansel Adams once said, that commercialism has robbed photography of its dignity, clarity, and effectiveness?

CUNNINGHAM: I don't think so. I think some commercial photography is very good. It should still be looked on as commercial photography, however.

BC: Should a photographer be able to learn from commercial work and then apply it to his personal work?

CUNNINGHAM: I think a commercial photographer should stay where he belongs. I've rarely seen a good commercial photographer who could do anything else well. Usually the necessity or desire to make a living does something to their work. What else did Ansel say?

BC: *In 1944 he suggested a severe licensing control of professional photographers and a firm guild organization among creative artists and professionals. I assume that was to prevent a rampage of shutterbugs. Like automobile drivers.*

CUNNINGHAM: You can't control the public. That would be fascist. Ansel has had the world as his own for quite a while.

BC: *Is that why you took that 1953 photograph of him like a titan on a mountain top?*

CUNNINGHAM: No, I was a still photographer on a movie being made on Ansel. He never gave any recognition to the work I did on that movie until 1976 when he used a portrait I took of him in his big hat for the cover of one of his books. In that portrait I took him straight-on to show his crooked nose. He's grown accustomed to it now, but for twenty years he used a profile shot that didn't show the crookedness.

BC: *In portraiture do you ever try to emphasize an aspect of a person that is true but unflattering to the person?*

CUNNINGHAM: I don't try to show anything that any person might feel is derogatory. I try to capture what I think is their natural self. I don't think you can hide deficiencies, if you call them deficiencies—I just call them differences.

BC: *I understand that when you photograph people you ask them to think of the nicest thing they can think of.*

CUNNINGHAM: Sometimes I do, sometimes I don't. One of my very best subjects was photographed heiling Hitler. It was a girl in my first book called Helena. She was an Olympic fencer.

BC: *Do you interview your portrait subjects before photographing them?*

CUNNINGHAM: I try to get acquainted with them before the first sitting.

BC: *What are the primary requirements of a good portrait photographer?*

CUNNINGHAM: You must be able to gain an understanding at short notice and at close range of the beauties of character, intellect, and spirit, so that you can draw out the best qualities and make them show in the face of the sitter.

BC: *You worked in Hollywood shooting portraits of movie stars for* Vanity Fair. *How did your approach work there?*

CUNNINGHAM: I told them I only wanted to photograph ugly men.

BC: *Ugly?*

CUNNINGHAM: Because first of all they would look better in a picture than they really are. They aren't as vain and they don't complain. Well, Cary Grant wasn't exactly ugly ... I did James Cagney though. He described me as the only photographer who hadn't blown a fuse in his house. The reason I didn't blow a fuse was that I photographed him out in the sunlight with his shirt off. He was making a picture about a prizefighter at the time. I also shot Wallace Beery next to his Bellanca airplane. He was wearing a dirty leather jacket, spotted gray flannels, and patent leather pumps. He had a toothache but behaved well.

BC: *Could you talk about beauty and its relationship to photography?*

CUNNINGHAM: To worship beauty for its own sake is narrow. One surely cannot derive from it the aesthetic pleasure which comes from finding beauty in the commonest things.

BC: *Where do you photograph in your apartment?*

CUNNINGHAM: Anywhere. I tear a few things to pieces, move things around. I don't photograph outdoors anymore, except a few portraits. If anyone can walk up my thirty-one stairs, I get them to come here and I shoot them with a 4x5 on Polaroid and when I think I've got what I like, I let them go. It's very nice, quick, and easy.

BC: *But this is your studio here—just your livingroom?*

CUNNINGHAM: When I work indoors my work is not really studio work. I like to do people as they really are in a room, not the way they would look if they were on a stage, unless of course they were stage people. Then I would go to the theater and photograph them with stage lighting. I'm not like Karsh— he's done some great portraits but now they all seem to have this back-lit halo formula.

I photographed Minor White under my porch against an old branch that I cut off. Everything was natural. That's the way he was, but not the way he looks now. He has long hair now. He likes to look like that. You see, he's the world's photographic guru. Well, I'm not.

BC: *Do you agree with his ideas on the interpretation of photographs?*

CUNNINGHAM: Minor once used my portrait of the painter Morris Graves for a class he teaches in what he calls "reading a photograph." Of course, personally, I don't believe in teaching how to read a photograph. I believe each person should learn for himself. What Minor does in teaching, I don't know. But he gave this photograph of mine to his students who knew nothing about Graves as a person. They wrote down their ideas about the man in the portrait and Minor sent them to me and asked me to comment on each impression.

I said I believed he had more poets in his class than photographers. The remarkable thing was that they did pick out a lot of stuff that is like Morris.

BC: *Why did you superimpose two negatives for your later portrait of Graves?*

CUNNINGHAM: I had an extremely good reason for doing that. Morris Graves' house is built on a lake that was formed by an accident so that it is a big hole with no shore. I asked him to jump in the lake, and he wouldn't do that because he was afraid that he would look like a drowned rat, which he would have. So he took me around the lake and I photographed all the big dark shadows that I thought I could use to superimpose him against. I carry with me a huge piece of black velvet when I go to work in some place I'm not familiar with. I use the felt if I want to hide anything. I hung it from the eaves of the house where they were low and took him against it. Then I put the two negatives together.

BC : When did you develop the idea for this picture?

CUNNINGHAM: I decided it that minute. I wanted to photograph him standing up to his waist in the lake but he wouldn't tread water. When I superimposed the negatives, it worked out that his hand was right near a ripple in the water of the other negative. I called the photograph *Pentimento*, which is a painter's term for a painting that has had another painted over it. With time, the images of the underpainting show through. It does this in a different way in this photograph. I had the idea from a Lillian Hellman book with that title—*Pentimento*. There's one woman who tells the truth.

BC : When you photograph people, do you feel some sort of emotional exchange?

CUNNINGHAM: I can't guarantee it. Sometimes you don't feel at home with the people. I try to field the kind of people I can get along with. In my professional life as a portrait photographer, I never refused anybody, but very often I've been terrifically despondent; not always in my work, but in people's lack of acceptance of anything I did. Very often people can't face themselves. They can't live with the faces they were born with. It's not a nice occupation to try to please people with their own faces. I've only photographed one person who likes everything I've done of her, and I've photographed her for twenty years. Her name is Barbara Myers.

BC : Have you ever used models?

CUNNINGHAM: I don't like models. They're always models no matter what you do to them. I've only photographed paid models once, in 1910. But they were not real models—they just needed the money.

BC : And the people who posed for other early works like The Vision *were all friends of yours?*

CUNNINGHAM: That woman I used in *The Vision* shared my

49

studio with me when I was young and I'm trying to get her to pose for me now. She's my age. She's sick though, having trouble with her eyes, which I had also. General physical disintegration.

BC: You've remained close all these years?

CUNNINGHAM: No, only by letter. I haven't seen her in fifty years. She lives in Reno.

BC: Will that be a shock, seeing her after so long a time?

CUNNINGHAM: How can you tell? It will be interesting, but it will be tough, because I won't want to look worse than she does. She complains in almost every letter and I have an idea she isn't well.

BC: Can we talk about your book on old age. Are the subjects friends of yours?

CUNNINGHAM: No. I don't have any friends who are as old as I am except for that woman from *The Vision*. I have a long list of doctors who give me names of people to photograph. The book is called *After 90*. I recently did a tattooed woman who was in hospital and now I'm looking for an American Indian because I've done enough women already. Women in old age are great camouflagers. They're all liars. They want to look better than they really are. They usually dress up when you go to photograph them. I even found a doctor like that the other day. My gracious, he had a handkerchief in his breast pocket. That's not done anymore! No one ever bothers with a beautifully folded handkerchief anymore.

BC: Why do you prefer black-and-white to color?

CUNNINGHAM: You have a better scale in it. You can do more elusive things with it. Color is so realistic. It's still tied to reality. A few people have done some good things with color, but mostly when they're more abstract, when the pictures are about color itself.

BC: What does quality in a print mean to you?

CUNNINGHAM: A broad range of darks and lights. The tendency of the present time is too much dark and too much light.

BC: *What about grain in a photograph?*

CUNNINGHAM: I'll tell you a very nice little story about that. My son Rondal said to me, "You can make just as good enlargements from a 35mm as you can from a 2¼." I said I didn't agree with him and he said, "You're standing too close, that's all." I think that's a good answer. I don't like very large prints though.

BC: *Would you say your subject matter has been determined to a certain extent by your choice of camera?*

CUNNINGHAM: You choose your camera after your subject matter. I photograph anything that can be exposed to light. The reason during the twenties that I photographed plants was that I had three children under the age of four to take care of so I was cooped up. I had a garden available and I photographed them indoors. Later when I was free I did other things. I've never felt limited by my equipment.

BC: *You've never used small cameras?*

CUNNINGHAM: No.

BC: *How many prints do you make of a photograph?*

CUNNINGHAM: I don't count. There is no reason to number a photograph. It's different with an engraving because the burr wears off the plate but if you treat a negative right you can make many prints.

BC: *What about the permanence of your prints?*

CUNNINGHAM: Talk to somebody else. I don't give a damn. The only thing that will destroy platinum prints is fire.

BC: *I know you use Polaroid film in a big camera, but have you tried the SX-70?*

CUNNINGHAM: I think they're all rummy. Not a decent one ever made.

BC: *Are you motivated by a strong ego?*

CUNNINGHAM: I won't bother you with thoughts on myself. I'm not impulsive and I don't think I'm the greatest ever. I just want to work for my own satisfaction.

BC: *How do you deal with criticism of your work?*

CUNNINGHAM: If anyone I ever photographed disliked my work, I'd throw it in the wastebasket in front of them and say nothing. I will not defend anything. I'm not really interested in what people are saying now about my work. Wait a hundred years. You'll never hear of me then. The scene will be relieved of one object more.

BC: *How have you been affected by fame?*

CUNNINGHAM: A photographer came to me recently and wanted to photograph me and put my face on a T-shirt. I said, "I'm going to make it hard for you because I want a shirt for all my enemies." Putting my face on a T-shirt . . . I call that decadent, don't you? It is not an honor to be on a T-shirt.

I was on Jimmy Carter's, I mean Johnny Carson's show. That's supposed to be an honor, but it isn't when you think about what he does every night. Sometimes he gets famous people on there and destroys them, but you see *I* destroyed *him.* I took the show away from him completely. He didn't open his mouth so I just kept popping. I turned away and talked to the boy next to me who was a comedian and he was very nice and agreeable. In fact, all my friends thought I did just the right thing to Johnny Carson. He's not a bad fellow. Well-liked, I understand, but I never stay up to watch him.

BC: *How has being a woman affected your life as a photographer?*

CUNNINGHAM: I'm a photographer, not a woman. I don't think it makes any difference if you just work. I was never treated badly. I was in this before the feminist movement began, although I did see the suffragette gals at Hyde Park Corner and believed they were right. I believe in equal pay for equal work and, as far as I know, I've got it. If you're determined and can do good work, then I think you can put it over without being in a collection of women. I don't like the way they roar around although I did visit the new Women's Building in Los Angeles. I had a show there once and it was very unprofitable. Since they had so much space I thought it would be nice to show with a friend of mine from New Mexico who was a man, but they told me they didn't show work by men. I don't feel that's right at all. It's going too far.

BC: How do you feel about the work being done by younger photographers today?

CUNNINGHAM: They're scrambling for themselves. I don't like the work of any young persons. I think at the schools they have a pattern—they copy from each other.

BC: What are your feelings about teaching photography?

CUNNINGHAM: I think it is overdone. A master's degree is a waste of time. Once you learn how to print and develop, you should be on your own. They would do better learning about literature or philosophy—a well-rounded education.

I don't believe in using class situations with models and set-ups. I tell all my students that whatever you do in class, put it in the wastebasket. You aren't arranging it—it's set up for you. When you have five or six other students shooting the same set-up, it's not yours.

BC: What advice would you give to a young photographer?

CUNNINGHAM: It's a big waste of time. It seems like the whole world has turned into photographers. I can't think it's reasonable.

BC: What do you think of the prices being paid today for photographs?

CUNNINGHAM: It's exaggerated. Everything has gone up excessively.

BC: It seems to get harder and harder to say who is a "real" photographer and who is just a trend.

CUNNINGHAM: Well who knows? I don't think art historians help you very much. Beaumont Newhall now has a grant to re-do his first book. This will be the third edition of it. More than twenty years ago at Eastman House I told him how Edward S. Curtis had been neglected. He made a note of this in his notebook but in the second edition he only added maybe one sentence more about Curtis. Nothing more. He didn't feel the influence of Curtis but I did. I thought of him as a great photographer. He was forgotten, and now when they dig him up they show bad reproductions.

BC: Your own career has spanned seventy-five years. Which of your photographs is your favorite?

CUNNINGHAM: The one I'm going to take tomorrow.

Cornell Capa

Cornell Capa was born in 1918, in Budapest, Hungary. He began photography at the age of nineteen, working in Paris in the darkrooms of his brother, the famous photojournalist Robert Capa, and Cartier-Bresson. In 1946 he joined Magnum, the photographers' cooperative they had helped to found, and was a member until 1954—a year marked by the deaths of his brother and Werner Bischof, a close friend and photographer, both killed while on assignments. Two years later, another colleague, David Seymour ("Chim") was killed at Suez.

For the next twenty years, Capa's work was channeled in two directions. On one hand there was his personal career, covering the world as a freelance photographer, doing assignments for *Life* magazine, and being the sole photographer for nine books and photographic editor of thirteen others. On the other hand, there was the work to establish something in his brother's memory.

To this end, in 1958, along with his mother and Seymour's sister, Capa established the Robert Capa–David Seymour Photographic Foundation in Israel. Its objectives were "to promote the understanding and appreciation of photography as a medium for revealing the human condition." Then in 1966, Capa helped establish the Capa–Bischof–Seymour Photographic Fund.

PHOTOGRAPH BY DICK SWIFT

By 1971, the fund had become, in Capa's words "a museum without walls—with exhibits, lectures, books and slides" and the finding of a permanent home became his primary objective. In 1974, a suitable site was found—Audubon House—a neo-Georgian mansion in New York City that had formerly been the headquarters of the National Audubon Society. Seven months later, the International Center of Photography opened, dedicated to "the appreciation of photography as the most important art/communication form of the 20th Century with the capacity to provide images of man and his world that are both works of art and moments of history."

Capa's own work includes *Margin of Life* (about over-population and hunger) and *Farewell to Eden* (on the Amahuaca Indians of Peru). Among the books he has edited are *Jerusalem: City of Mankind* and the *Concerned Photographer* books.

There was a look of dismay on Cornell Capa's face as we came through the outer door of his office on the top floor of the International Center of Photography. Then his expression changed to one of resignation: the interview could not be avoided. He sat down behind his desk and eyed us critically as we set up the tape recorder.

Cornell Capa is a powerful-looking man with thick gray hair

57

*and the dark, alert eyes of a Picasso owl. On the day we inter-
viewed him, he was dressed casually in a pullover sweater and
khaki pants, and smoked one cigar after another, filling the sun-
lit room with sails of smoke.*

*Throughout the interview, a large black poodle named Yofi
interrupted us continually, passing back and forth between the
offices and forcing Capa to rise several times from his chair to open
the door. "Yofi means 'exuberant' in Hebrew," explained Capa.*

*There is very little of himself that Capa wants to promote. He is
a man motivated by a concern, a cause, and it is difficult to leave
him without feeling affected by this. At the beginning of the interview, a series of mostly biographical questions brought no more
than routine answers; but when we moved on to the topic of photojournalism—its power to effect change, its growing exposure—it
was as if the big man had woken up.*

*After talking for a long time, he had to leave to attend a meeting
but he asked that we stay. Forty-five minutes later he came back
and picked up where he had left off with equal if not more enthusiasm.
We talked for another hour and a half, finishing only when he had
to leave in order to meet a Canadian photographer who had come
to New York to meet him. It was seven o'clock by then and Cornell
Capa's day was far from over.*

*JD : In 1972, I understand you were called in by the State of New
York to take pictures of Attica. This was after the uprising?*

CAPA: Yes. I knew one of the Attica Commission lawyers and
he understood the notions of why photography is a witness,
an *eyewitness*, and that a visual perception of what was going
on by someone who knows how to see would matter; so a year
after the uprising he asked me to go and spend some time there
to find out what had happened. Since I did that, and as a result
of it, I was part of the Commission. I was on the witness stand
with my pictures. Perfectly in line with everything I have ever
done.

JD : And quite symbolic.

CAPA: Perfectly right, because I was able to see and perceive.
That's what we're about. It was a perfect use of my capacity
as one who sees.

58

JD : As one who sees, are you ever disillusioned with the real effect your images have or don't have?

CAPA: The disillusionment is very simple: wars are still being fought. But on the other hand, every philosopher, every revolutionary and every manifesto writer and anyone who has had a theory of government, could also jump off the bridge with me. I'd have lots of company. Why should I be discouraged because the world is a hard place to bring into some kind of living rhythm? Why should I stop? Why should I cease fighting with what I can fight with just because it's difficult to achieve? The minute you give in, it's hopeless, you might as well jump off the bridge. It's just that simple.

As for the capacity to affect—we do. With all the arguments and discussions about the Vietnam war, what did the visual image do? It ended the war. I don't have a question about that. Never mind that we did it by choking you, by making you so sensitized that you threw your hands up and shrieked, "Enough, I don't want anymore. It is too much." Fine. When it became too much, it stopped. Johnson couldn't go on anymore. How did it happen? The nation had too much of it. Thank you. Lovely. It worked.

JD : What would you say is your greater contribution to photography—would it be the founding of ICP (The International Center of Photography) or your own personal work?

CAPA: Nothing is unconnected. My first work as a photographer coincided with the birth of the major picture magazines. I was in France in 1936 just before *Match* and *Picture Post* made their appearance. My brother Robert, Cartier-Bresson, and David Seymour were working at the time for a daily newspaper (*Ce Soir*), working in an experimental way because news photographs and the way they were being used were very stilted. It was all 4x5 with reporters telling photographers, "Get that picture." But these three photographers were experimenting with the 35mm camera in their own way. They were shooting candid pictures of events, which developed into the magazine format of sequential story-telling.

So my initial involvement in photography coincided with the experimental movements of that period. It's very interesting, of course, to compare that time to 1975 and the disappearance of the same cycle. The birth of ICP, as such, followed the end of that cycle, and now experimental photography involves other kinds of experiments. I don't even dare to categorize what the new forms are. They are certainly not for publication, except for the personal expression kind of books—thirty to forty-eight pages of textless essays of a sort, but basically those are single pictures more than connected pieces. Of course, there is the so-called "conceptual" work, all kinds of things which are not necessarily flat prints at all; videotapes, and combination videotapes with audio experiences. So I don't know where photography is today, or where it is going. One thing is definite, though; one thing began with my beginnings and it has ended now. Money is involved too, because photographers have to make a living somewhere, so how do you make a living? At one time it was publishing or publication. Currently I think the major impetus is to be sold, to have your prints sold.

JD : You mentioned your brother, Cartier-Bresson and David Seymour; wasn't your start in photography printing their work?

CAPA: Yes. That was the period that I've told you about. They were working for a newspaper. I just got out of school and went to Paris from Hungary. And what that period gave me, of course, is to a great extent missing from the current scene: to apprentice with someone and work in a laboratory for specific kinds of people, like those three.

When I came to America I went to work for PIX, which is an agency my brother was connected with, and I worked in a darkroom even when I came here. I was doing work for a group of people, including Eisenstaedt and ten or twelve other photographers of more or less note, which gave me a great comparative background. In that way printing is just like reading. You can read and learn nothing, or you can absorb a great deal. You can learn a great amount about composition, approach, and you can find out what a person is all about because you are with the photographer as a person in personal contact with him while printing.

Eisenstaedt didn't print very much himself, but he knew how to print, and would very carefully control the printing that I did for him. The same with the others. It was a very skilled period. If a photographer did not do his own printing for time-saving reasons, he would still know exactly what he wanted to bring out of the print. And if the print was not brilliant enough, dark enough, this enough or that enough, he would force the printer to go back and do it again. I learned a great deal about the individual's approach to his photography, or to his own printing techniques, compositions, and all the rest of it. The apprentice system, whether it was direct or semi-direct, gave me a good chance to work very closely with a number of people whose work obviously had affected or interested me. Those who did not interest me, I'd just skim through them, pass them by.

I worked at *Life* during the Margaret Bourke-White period, and all the early *Life* types: Otto Hagel, tremendous technically brilliant photographer, and Gjon Mili and Eliot Elisofon, who printed their own work, were all around and one would get fantastic insights from watching their work which, at that time, was all experimental. Technological revolutions proliferated during those last thirty years. Technically, great advances were made in lighting systems and the uses of special lenses. So my own development was very much affected by technical brilliance and use of all kinds of equipment, cameras and lights, light sources, and printing techniques. Simultaneously, of course, came the story forms—the first issue of *Life* with Bourke-White's cover about the dam, and unemployment, etc., etc. The beginning of the photographic essay was upon us. So besides the technical developments, there was this photographic narration, short story, elongated essay, news coverage that grabs you, tells you the guts of the story. There was no consideration given to an exhibition and nobody to buy a print. Now, suddenly, the news story is not the thing; the print is, and the difference is right there. And that difference only came to fruition, really, in 1970, 1972.

JD : Is that distinction important to you?

CAPA: It's tremendously important, but what's really important is that it is bound to affect the direction of what's happening now. It's very obvious that we were involved in informing people—informing and affecting an audience. At the present time, however, you're appealing to some other sensibility. I don't know who's going to describe to me or characterize anaesthetic sensibility, an individual one, that will move me to the point of spending $150 to $350 to buy that one image, when I could have bought *Life* magazine for 10¢ with 150 pages of such images.

To go back to the original question, though, the circumstances are so radically different in intention. The intention to communicate and inform, and to bring the world to you in some new narrative form for almost no expense, to buy a magazine for 10¢, was a fantastic thing. It's like looking at television now. Looking at television doesn't cost you any money except your initial investment to buy the set, and then the world's images are coming at you; you can be entertained twenty-four hours a day, subsidized by the advertisers. The advertisers subsidized the magazines; for 10¢ you could get this world of photography brought to you. Against that, for a single print that I may want to own and have on my wall, I have to spend as much as $400. It's the difference of a whole world!

Strangely enough, until 1970 or so, you did not find very many people who were ready to spend any amount of money on a print. I have an interesting illustration of that: my brother's "Spanish Soldier" photograph, one of the most widely printed images of our time. Well, in 1967 when I had it at an exhibition at the Riverside Museum, we made some prints available for sale, in order to pay for the exhibition. It was put on sale as a master print for $60. It was available through the Museum of Modern Art since 1950. They bought a couple of copies for their permanent collection, and when they sold one, they would ask the artist to give a new one to replace it. So it's been at the MOMA since 1950. It's been available at the Riverside Museum. It's been available here since we opened. I think we sold five prints during that period. From 1950 to 1975, five original prints were purchased.

Nobody wanted the most famous, the most outstanding, the most any kind of photograph. There was simply no market for it. The market is for some other reason. I can't even attempt to explain why Ralph Gibson's *Feather in a Lady's Behind* sells for $350. I can't follow that.

JD : And you don't think this has changed at all?

CAPA: No. There is no change. The kind of buying that's going on is erratic, you have lots of different fish. There may be some institutional buying into permanent collections which is brand new, and collector buying which is mainly nineteenth-century prints. I don't know how much contemporary buying exists. By whom? I have no answers to these questions. I only have a few examples to know what does not sell.

JD : And the market that exists may not be permanent.

CAPA: The point is that once there was no market at all. I don't know what suddenly got all of these people interested. There is a break of some nature, quite inexplicable, or unexplained, to me. One would hope for logical, progressive, educated change where people learn more and slowly buy more. Unfortunately, it didn't happen that way.

JD : When did you first take your own photographs?

CAPA: I did it simultaneously with my darkroom work, during my PIX period, but actually my real picture-taking period began after the war. I did do some picture taking during my air force days, in photo-intelligence, and some public-relations photography which was a five-finger exercise, but after the war I joined *Life*'s staff from which point I've been steadily photographing.

JD : You first went to Israel in 1967. Was that when the Concerned Photography Fund was born?

CAPA: Several different things were born. In 1960, we did a Capa/"Chim" photographic foundation for Israel because they both had many friends there and they both photographed the birth of the country. My mother and Seymour's sister wanted to create something that would encourage personal, committed photography in Israel. After that, it became the Capa, Bischof, Seymour Memorial etc., a real tongue breaker, and it was very limiting because it was a memorial for three people, which it was never meant to be. So when we did the Concerned Photographer exhibition, I changed its name to indicate a tradition. It became much clearer to me that it was more involved in a tradition of photography—involvement with life—than a memorial to three people.

Again, to get another perspective, Concerned Photography became a symbol for a concerned decade—everybody jumped on to the use of *concerned*. Concerned Citizens for anything.

63

It was so successful that it diminished my own use. I felt I was plagiarizing myself. It just played itself out, simply because it was taken up by everybody else. If I could have put a copyright on the word in fact to describe a direction in photography which would remain its own signal, I would have no problem with it now because to be concerned about the world is as wide as the ocean; it means a depth of involvement and all the other things that go with it. I wouldn't have changed it, but it became an overused word, which was very interesting because, of course, it touched the nerve of our time.

JD : You also mentioned once that concern *was a word which could not be translated properly into any other language.*

CAPA: It couldn't. We tried the Italian—*fotographia impregnata.* It sounds like you're pregnant. And *engagiert photographer, engagiert* means a lot of things—you're engaged because maybe you're hired. There is no good translation for it, so it had to remain the Concerned Photographer in any language.

JD : Do you think that the concept of the Concerned Photographer and the audience that this will attract is something particularly American?

CAPA: I don't think so. But the word *concerned* communicates a special thing to American–English speaking people. Even in England you would have a different translation already—we don't share the same levels of understanding. It doesn't mean that one is higher or lower than the other, but it's cultural. It doesn't translate.

We are stuck with a lot of things. News photography covers a multitude of things, documentary photography covers the same—they both deal with people and events. They are very wide statements, wide generalizations that we can get by with.

As umbrellas go, there is much more that could be called "Concerned Photography," but it became counter-productive because everybody would start joking about: "Well, am I concerned enough?" The joke wears thin after the first two seconds. "Yes, I'm a concerned photographer," says he, "I'm concerned about money." So what do you do? Eventually, it became very counter-productive because the discussion didn't go anywhere. It has a punch line, and either you laugh or you grin, or you shrug your shoulders. It doesn't lead to discussion. Eventually one could not really talk about the meanings of photography very seriously under that heading because the conversation would end with a joke. Somebody else's joke.

JD : I was wondering about the reactions in different countries. The Concerned Photographer exhibit was in Tokyo in . . .?

CAPA: 1968.

JD : And what was the effect?

CAPA: It's very difficult. One fantastic part, first of all, was the personality cult. The Japanese were very impressed by my brother, they knew so much about him, and he was a figure, so they were very excited about looking at his camera—like a moonrock.

The picture which was really interesting, in terms of reaction, was the French collaborator woman who is being marched through the streets of France, with a baby in her arms and a shaven head. We put on a caption like *Chartres, 1944,* and all those people looking at the picture didn't understand it. Culturally there is no understanding why you would shave a woman's head. In the Japanese view, there's no cultural equivalent for that kind of guilt. They don't know what the guilt was, so they looked at the picture blankly. I thought it spoke to everybody. It didn't.

JD : When the fund for Concerned Photography took off, did that more or less curtail your own personal photography?

CAPA: Well, one terrible thing that I did to myself, of course, is that for the last twenty years more or less, since 1954, since my brother's death, Seymour's death in 1956, and everything else, and then getting involved with Magnum's fate for a while, I used up all my time. I used a twenty-four hour day and fell into a seven-day-week routine. The way I managed to do these things was that I did my public service in my extra time. I did my photography in my own time. I would use my time at nights and weekends etc. to do all the things I wanted to do. Eventually I got to the point where I'm always using all the time I have. It really doesn't answer the question terribly well.

A fairly representative example is 1974. I published three different kinds of books. My own book *Margin of Life*, one on *Jerusalem* which I sparked and photographed part of, and the *Concerned Photographer 2* book which I conceived and edited. They really demonstrate my three ways of doing things. I used the large notion of the concerned photographer with individual achievements summed up in a life's work in portfolios; take a large subject like Jerusalem as a concept and take part in it as a photographer, and shape its outline and gather the photographers who become part of explaining, in their own way, photographically, what the subject is about; and the third one is my own personal photography on a particular subject, which is *Margin of Life*.

One thing is the same in all of them though, and I think that's kind of significant any which way—all these projects utilize the work of the photographer as a statement of his own. It's not the concept of *The Family of Man* where an editor takes pieces, makes something out of it using visual images to express the editor's ideas. The point is, in all the things I have done as an organizer of projects in which I take the editor's part, or where I participate as a photographer, the individual photographer gets a chance to make his own statement. Every book that I can show you has a comparatively full statement by each photographer. Six in the *Concerned Photographer*, eight in the *Concerned Photographer 2*, twenty-one people in *Jerusalem, City of Mankind*—each one writes his piece, and the layout that follows is a faithful enough expression with sixteen, eighteen or twenty pages of his own interest in life. I'm very much for the capacity of a photographer to express what he wants to express. I think that's what a concerned photographer really is, because they express their preoccupation in whatever they're interested in. Whatever the subject is, it's their own statement about it. I think that's exactly where the depth of involvement matters.

We just received a form letter invitation for the Fourth International Exhibition of Photography about "children." This editor has produced three other previous exhibitions; he asked everybody to send in pictures. He already knows what he wants. He picks five Ken Heymans, and three of somebody else and two others and puts together his mosaic. It's his bag, it's his exhibit—these are *Family of Man*-type exhibitions where he has a notion of what he wants to say with pictures.

Then he tries to find the images to fit his theory. Well, I'm not doing that. In everything I have done, it did not go that way, and I think that's really the major importance in an attitude to a photographer's work: photographers work as individuals, and the work of photography is in the sense of illuminating some dark corners of life. If you did the same thing with Arbus's work, in twenty-four pages you could certainly take out the best images that she has done in that particular milieu. A hundred and sixty pages of all her images multiply to the same point, they all add up to the same statement. But you can have it in a concentrated form, or amply diffused. Take them all, or pick the one you like. The job of the editor is to try to arrive at the essence—that's the role that I have taken, to concentrate it somewhat.

JD : In a previous interview, you said when ICP started here you were not interested in showing the work of people like Minor White or Ansel Adams.

CAPA: I didn't say that.

JD : That they had the art galleries to go to.

CAPA: I didn't quite say that either. I hope I would have said the same thing I say now. I have less and less interest in showing the work of people who have an ample platform somewhere else. My interest is in showing work that would not be shown otherwise. It still remains very much the same. Originally, there wasn't a great interest to show photojournalists' work anywhere. The Metropolitan and MOMA didn't take that route for whatever reasons—I'm not particularly ready to discuss it, it doesn't matter—but photojournalists' work, the storytelling work, not the single picture of great beauty, was not very much in vogue before the galleries came, and it is not in vogue since the galleries came. Nothing changed. So at this point I feel less guilt, if any, for not showing that work because they have ample opportunity to have their work seen, shown and bought. I don't have any feeling about my real super-obligation to add one more platform to those that exist, while continuing to cut out what was cut out all the time.

JD : I was wondering to what extent your concept of concerned

67

photography can be expanded; because you said once: "A couple of years ago, I would not have considered Eliot Porter to be a concerned photographer, but suddenly our forests are slipping away," and then he becomes a concerned photographer.

CAPA: There is no question about a lot of things. There is no question about my own growth of perception of what is and what isn't, and everything is eventually, so that's one thing. Second thing, which I think is terribly important in this particular place, I also don't think exhibition is the last word.

During the last five years, three years at New York University, and for four semesters here, I originated a lecture series format for photographers. I have now given a platform to 200 photographers, minimally, to show and speak on their own work, and I think that particular kind of presentation is just as important, just as powerful, just as everything else, as photographs on the wall. And the 200 people who lectured in this series embrace every kind of an individual discipline that you ever want to consider. So, as far as I'm concerned, it's not only the wall, the exhibition form that's ultimate. It's one more form.

BC: So this involves the photographer as an individual much more.

CAPA: Each time, each time, each time.

BC: And in the Concerned Photographer *books, this time, the writing is obviously about the photographs.*

CAPA: If you look at certain things, some of the forms and formats seem the same, but they aren't. In the *Concerned Photographer* books themselves, besides the introduction which often speaks about the photographer in an abbreviated description, loaded with a lot of their quotations, when you go into the back of the books, instead of having camera information, there is always the photographer's narrative of what it's all about. You may not have noticed it particularly because there wasn't much spotlight put on why it was different—it's for you to discover. You can look at the photographs by themselves with only date and place identification and appreciate that quality and the way they follow each other—it spells out their area of interest—or you can look at the picture itself, alone. But if you

68

read the beginning statement and if you read the information in the back of what they're really saying about their work, you really learn what motivates these men apart from the images that come out of it.

Of course when you talk to this new group of photographers today, they all talk about their "pieces." I mean they all become terribly artistic because "my piece is bought." We never talked about "my piece being bought." It was: the story had an impact because we wanted to tell you something. We wanted to inform you, we wanted to shock you, we wanted to have you appreciate whatever it is and do something, make you act. It's a whole other thing, and I hope it is going to remain in all different forms. I'm not trying to insist on the still photograph. There's television and film—the film makers and *cinema verité*, and all the rest of them are direct descendants, both in form and content, and in making you react in some very strong kind of a manner, and this is the tradition I'm talking about.

BC: How important was the 35mm camera to that?

CAPA: Tremendously. Equally, you can see what is happening now when television cameras, video cameras are becoming portable. It's the same route. It's all the same.

JD: Do you think there comes a point where, being continually exposed to images of horror and violence, people become desensitized?

CAPA: I don't. All these things become very poor arguments because I think you have to go back to words and pictures. Since when did you get tired of reading words just because there are so many books that you say "Aaagh, forget it, I'm not going to read a word again"? It all depends what you are reading. And I think it's the same with photographs. We are exposed so much to commonplace photography that it needs a greater imagery, a greater subtlety, a greater anything to engage you. Also, I think you may be interested in what I have to say as an author whose views are different. You trust me—I care about something that interests you. Take columnists, for instance: Why do you read Scotty Reston? You can read all the Associated Press stories and get it all. But you read Reston, because he's doing something with words and mind and intelligence and whatever it is. He has a wonderful use of language that makes me want to read what the hell he has to say. And I think in photography, it is and will remain the same.

JD: Then you don't believe that the photographer should be completely impersonal or unbiased?

CAPA: First of all, no artist can be. I cannot conceive of having an impersonal image because all the artist photographers are talking about private visions and personal images and all the rest of it. So I really don't see that argument at all. I cannot see it because a documentary photographer chooses everything, from where he went to the moment he shoots; from what his interest is, to what moment he selects and how he puts it together. This is as personal a vision as any personal vision can be, and it cannot be objective. If it is objective, then he has a very difficult time to engage anybody in looking at it. If it has no personality of any nature, what's the point?

But these are very specious arguments. Very few people read an Associated Press dispatch which gives you facts only, supposed facts, only. It's a whole other thing than going into the why and how and all the rest of it. Go beyond and behind the facts—that's what interpretations are, and that's where everything begins. I think that photography, and using photography as visual language, has all the earmarks of the other language, the written.

BC: Doesn't the Concerned Photographer have a special responsibility then?

CAPA: Any photographer does. "I didn't know the gun was loaded." To me, the most incredibly wonderful thing is what happens when sometimes you really don't know what happens. Eddie Adams was the greatest example of this, shooting that picture of the police chief shooting the Viet Cong in the street. If he was a Concerned Photographer, he may not have taken that picture because he would have attempted to stop the policeman from shooting the man, at which point he would have prevented the dissemination of a most important photograph which made everybody else realize what the Vietnam fighting was all about. So without thinking about it, without being concerned about the effect, etc., just by photographing the scene, doing his job, he has done his great act.

JD : I read that he was angry afterwards about the way the picture was represented.

CAPA: I don't know what you mean.

JD : That he felt it has been taken out of context.

CAPA: He wasn't angry. Again, discussions go on forever. He came to one of the symposia I ran a long time ago and he told the story of how it happened—what he could do, what he couldn't do, why he took it, and the rest of it; and he did not even know when he took it what an important picture it was until he saw it reprinted all over the world. The war stopped two or three years later, and somehow everybody kept on talking about that picture that made everybody sit up. But if it was out of context, then it proves the point that he did not have to be critically concerned about the picture. *It* did the job.

BC : How much does the viewer need to be told though? There may be a most dramatic picture of a policeman beating up a young student and the person is in actuality a murderer.

CAPA: You can't legislate this. You can't legislate what is true and what is false, and what is out of context. This is not out of context, that picture was not out of context. The viciousness of that particular war will stand on its own in the history books, because we never saw a thing like that happen.

In Vietnam, because Asians allowed themselves to be photographed without realizing the impact photography could make, it just became an open field. It was marvelous for photographers to be able to see the ugliest face of war. People who were more concerned about their own image in the Western culture could never photograph those scenes because they would never be let near enough. A second side is that possibly the Germans would not be as insensitive to others, to a Frenchman, as Vietnamese were to Vietnamese. But it's a cultural situation, and there they didn't understand the role of the press, didn't understand what this meant.

Another thing which is interesting: Ron Haeberle, who did

the photographs of My Lai, was at the symposium the same night as Eddie Adams, talking about his photographs. Duncan and some other people sort of asked him, accused him, whatever the circumstances were, "How come you never photographed any of the soldiers shooting the victims? You only saw the bodies, you never saw the thing really being committed." And he said: well, he wouldn't have lived very long because his fellow soldiers would have known, would have realized; but the Vietnamese soldier torturing a fellow Vietnamese did not have any of the same feeling about the impropriety and had no sense of how he would appear. It's really a lack of appreciation of the role of the press, the whole cultural lag and all the rest of it.

I just read in today's *Time* of a public execution in Nigeria, and the whole scene was described—your hair stands up. And why didn't we see any pictures of that? Because since they are more sophisticated about mass media, and world media, they do it without cameras. It's getting wise to the ways of bad publicity. It's the appreciation of what a camera can and will do. Through Telstar, it's here tomorrow morning or tonight, and the next day we shut off the armaments. Something happens. The U.N. meets in emergency session and something else happens. The power of visual communication is tremendous.

JD : Do you think that the photographer today has to watch out for people who are learning to manipulate the media?

CAPA: It hasn't changed any. It just became more sophisticated on every level. I agree with what you said before—I think we have to be much smarter, each one of us. . . . Smart is not exactly the right adjective, but it's a sophisticated thing to know how you use and how you are being used, being saturated with images.

BC : Do you think that ICP has influenced the younger photographers?

CAPA: Without a doubt. I have no question about it. If you come backwards, let's talk about outlets to show your work. If you can't show it here and be noticed aside from any commercial reason, where can you show it? So the encouragement of knowing that there is such a place for this kind of work is important. Please remember that it's like a shot heard around the world. There's a repeat of this everywhere. Other places, other countries are doing it because of this. If tomorrow morning you only had galleries that sell photographs, and that was the only market for photographs, then everybody would take pictures that people would buy; but I already told you earlier that people don't buy certain kinds of pictures. If the only pictures that will be seen are those that are to be bought, then soon enough you will have a consumer photography market of old prints of the past century or of new prints which are unique creations made to order to be consumed.

JD: With some exceptions though, surely. Wouldn't Cartier-Bresson's work be as commercial as he wanted? And he is shown here.

CAPA: But you must start out with the intent of the work. Just to show the master of this kind of photography is encouragement for people to see that sort of work. But I did not show Cartier-Bresson's work as a retrospective, we showed it as a thematic show. Almost every exhibit at the Center is a thematic show. It's thematic by one person.

About your previous question about my own photography—we can go into that for a while because it's essential. I felt very strongly that there was a need for an institution of this nature, and for a recognition of past and current work. Again, my ideas were before the revolution of the galleries. It's been a twenty-year growth process. Anyway, speaking only in the greatest generalities, what the galleries are really very much involved in is showing and dispersing work. They are not concerned with education, collections and preservation of negatives and prints. The "gallery explosion" didn't change the need for a place like this. At that point, the pressure of showing changed, but the pressure of showing this kind of work did not change. Nobody has been rushing to show the kind of work that we show here, okay?

We were trying to get to something . . . my own work . . . anyhow, my feeling as a photographer. As far as I'm concerned, I'm quite satisfied with my own past photographic output. I have no personal pressure to produce new work at this particular time. In my sense of priorities, the creation of this place was much more important for photography than the continuation

73

of my own work for the moment. I can pick up whenever I want to. I have only interrupted my work for a while, until I can see that this thing is anchored, and from a personal growth point of view, not speaking of the administrative side of this, but of my own contact with the world of photography and photographers, there has been a tremendous personal growth factor. So whenever I pick up myself again as a photographer, I think I'm tremendously enriched in my own perspective on photography. I feel absolutely no personal loss of my own photographic work because I feel quite at ease with myself. As a photographer, I don't have this great ego thing that the world is passing me by, or if I don't do it, nobody will be able to see what there is. I'm fully aware that it's being done by others. Not necessarily the way I would do it, but it's done. And what's more important is that possibly because of my unique combination of talents—my past, everything else—it made me a good candidate to attempt to make this place happen. And since there weren't too many willing candidates about who would have attempted it and would actually manage to create the Center, I have no regrets or conflicting pressures that I must do this, I must do that. It's a very good period for me not to feel a loss and to have my energies at the high level so I can put everything together.

With photography, I have no pressure of ending or beginning. It's a continuous process for me. When I go back to my next project as a photographer, I will be much enriched. What I'm going through photographically right now is almost like my period when I was in a darkroom. I learned a great deal then, and I'm now learning a lot on a different level. It's the right time from every point of view. That was the question you asked way back.

JD : How long were you with Magnum for?

CAPA: I was with *Life* from '47 to '54, and then when my brother was killed, I joined Magnum.

JD : Would you say that the concept behind Magnum was working up to what you are doing now, here?

CAPA: In many, many ways. What becomes very evident in perspective is how the cycle began in 1947, and Magnum was concerned with the integrity of the photographer, respect for what he says, the documentary tradition, etc. Magnum today is different from the Magnum of 1947 entirely, and it stopped short for any number of sufficient reasons. It is doing much commercial work of one nature, and it did not continue its commitment to this kind of photography because of living conditions, market conditions, whatever you like. So where that stops short, this may have been its logical forward thrust, getting into a non-commercial, institutional kind of a framework for documentary, commentary photography. If I did not want to become a commercial photographer, if that was not the development, it's logical that this happened. The Magnum concept did not itself change—pursuit of great photographs of great events, involvement with mankind, all that. If those had continued, in one frame, and I had not had the pressure, the realization as I started to look into what happens to a photographer's work after he dies—how the group cannot take care of it sufficiently, how the individuals outside can't manage to handle it—this might not have been necessary. But individually, I started to look into each one of these things, and I took up those bits and pieces by making books and exhibitions of their work, and the lack of possibilities made me realize the need for an institution of this nature to do the things that were not developing anywhere else.

It makes no sense to live a life, living through and amassing a legacy of history and all the rest of it, to have all of it become unavailable. Having learned this, the pressure not to allow it to happen became one of the most important springs of why I am here. The most essential thing that I, or anyone, can accomplish is to have a functioning vital force that preserves and propels, that handles the past, present and future; and it has to be on a non-commercial basis.

JD : Do you feel that the passing of the big picture magazines made it easier to set up a place like this?

CAPA: What's curious, of course, is how photography did not die with the passing of *Life* and *Look* and *Saturday Evening Post* and *Collier's* and all the rest of it. Besides the other reasons, which are stupid reasons, corporate reasons and all of it, *Life* in the last few years was doomed to die because it didn't solve its problem—television made a challenge, and the picture magazine couldn't meet it by whatever it attempted; so the physical death of it was only a logical end after a number of years of faltering.

A new world is upon us in photography—television brought it in, and the death of the mass magazines has presaged a whole new development, the potential for a whole new development, and a new recognition.

If one spends one's energies toward the dissemination of documentary, commentary photography in a more impacted form—be it television, screen, multi-media, spoken and visual monographs, video cassettes or cable television—there are so many new ways of having more personalized and wider impact, and more powerful ways to get your ideas across than the magazine ever had. There's a tremendous new chance for photography and I think by having those doors closed, it just makes the movement forward and sideways in many directions, it makes it so much stronger. If *Life* had continued to exist, it wouldn't have pressured us into a whole new direction. I think it's better this way.

JD : Do you think there might have been a way that the magazines could have met the challenges presented at that time?

CAPA: Sometimes it's such a complicated process. Eventually I believe that television advertising competition (a *Life* page being as expensive as TV time) was a deterrent, because they found that television was more effective for sales. When you added the post office cost of mailing, and added that television came ten days sooner than *Life* would ever appear, the magazine became an outdated concept. With the new magazines, the advertising rates are minimal because of a focused audience. You pay for advertising for a circulation of 300,000, not ten million. It wasn't logical, it had to die.

JD : With these new formats that photography has, what do you see happening to the print, the craft of the print?

CAPA: Oh God, there are so many things involved, like in arts and crafts, all these arts and crafts courses, how to regain our own hands. Old printing techniques are relearned and all that. I don't have a great amount of concern about that particularly. I'm delighted to have those prints that were printed a hundred years ago—I admire them and I admire other people who are relearning them—but to me, photography is much more exciting in its capacity to inform, to enchant, to give you new things, than the physical making of a print. It's a nice historic notion, but if you give me a chance to tell my story better or to learn gum printing all over again, I can assure you I'm not going into the gum printing course.

JD: What I was aiming at was what is going to happen to the original print. I don't care how it's printed, but I'm sure it's done with care by the photographer. From magazines to television, the degree of distortion must be substantial, so we're talking about a level where the image becomes all important. Because how many people come to ICP in a year?

CAPA: We had a hundred thousand people in one year. But that's not my point really. When I go on television for a half-hour show, and show my *Margin of Life* work, I get NET or some other network, and you're dealing with multi-millions. Candice Bergen is doing some five-minute things on NBC in the morning. They're giving her a chance to show her photographic essays on subject A, B, C, D, and E and she's able to talk about it. Duncan did it in the convention in 1968. They gave him a five-minute spot as a photographer/commentator to find a subject at the convention, and he could photographically and verbally comment on what the subject was. He found that to be exciting. And suddenly a hundred million people looked and heard what he found. That's what I'm talking about.

JD: So the transience of an image being on television doesn't bother you because its effect is so great?

CAPA: The impact of it is so great, and at the same time he may have already done it in a book. At the same time it's already on a wall, in different museums and archives; at the same time it's being reprinted in digest form, some magazine takes ten pages they spread out. It's like a bomb that bursts. So photography is now done better and with more impact than it was done in the previous regime. It's upon us now. It's not a dream. As for the new generation, my God, we never had it that good. To get $5,000 grants from the National Endowment for the Arts at the drop of a hat. . . . Who got $5,000 before? From where? With no obligations! To make a good proposal for getting a grant? Delicious!

Elliott Erwitt

Elliott Erwitt was born a U.S. citizen in Paris, 1928. He became interested in photography while in high school and worked as a darkroom technician in a Hollywood studio. He moved to New York City in 1948 and worked taking portraits of authors for book jackets.

He was taken up by Edward Steichen who found him a job at the studio of Sarra, a commercial photographer. After that, Erwitt worked for Roy Stryker, formerly head of the Farm Security Administration Historical Division.

In 1951, Erwitt entered the army and was stationed in France. There he met his first wife, Lucienne. His pictures of her—pregnant, and with their newborn child—later became part of the *Family of Man* exhibit. In 1953 he joined Magnum and served as president there, fighting for the cause of the photographer's right to retain copyright over his own pictures.

Since then, Erwitt has had exhibitions in the major galleries and museums of America. He has published several books including *Photographs and Anti-Photographs*, and *Son of Bitch* (a book about dogs). In 1976 he completed a project for the town of Corning, New York, taking pictures of people from all walks of life to form a life-size mural.

We interviewed Elliott Erwitt at the East Side apartment of a friend of his at ten o'clock one night in February. Erwitt has a

reputation for a distinctive sense of humor and when we called him from the phone in the lobby, before anything had been said, Erwitt answered, "Speaking!" making the question "Is Mr. Erwitt there?" a little ridiculous. Whether he uses this joke as a test for interviewers or as random amusement, Erwitt's reception upstairs was equally stand-offish—a greeting of studied indifference.

Elliott Erwitt is a man of medium height and build with dark curly hair and brown eyes that seem to be continuously amused in a way that makes you unsure of whether it is with you or at you. His accent is hard to place, but seems to be a cross between New York and smoothed-over Irish—an odd thing for the son of a Russian Jew raised in Los Angeles.

Erwitt introduced us to his friend and offered us a drink as we sat down at the kitchen table where we set up for the interview. He was tired from shooting all day and made no pretense about letting us know we were keeping him up. "I'm going to be difficult" was his opening line, but a few minutes later he seemed to relax— as if we had passed some private test of his—and he seemed genuinely interested in the interview's outcome.

JD: The story is different in most of the sources we have read, but was your first work as a photographer doing publicity stills in Hollywood?

ERWITT: Yes, printing them. When I was a little boy.

JD: What studio was that for?

ERWITT: It wasn't a studio. It was a house that made prints for the studios. You know these signed photographs from the stars. For the fans who write in saying, "I love you, I love you." You send back a signed picture.

JD: How many of those would you print a day?

ERWITT: Thousands. I was just helping to process them.

JD: How did you get interested in becoming a photographer yourself?

ERWITT: It seemed like a reasonable way of making a living.

JD: Do you remember when you first got a camera?

ERWITT: I bought an old wetplate camera for a few dollars and started experimenting with it. I must have been about sixteen.

JD: And when you worked for Sarra?

ERWITT: Actually, that job was gotten for me by Steichen. He thought that I needed work, and indeed I did, so he called Valentino Sarra and told him that he had somebody who needed work. And anything that old Captain Steichen requested was generally done by anybody. Or else. . . .

JD: And you took pictures of authors for book jackets? I've seen the one of Mencken.

ERWITT: At the beginning I did a lot of that. Mencken was terrific. Mencken, Thomas Mann, Conrad Richter—lots of people. Mainly Knopf authors because I had a friend working for Knopf and he used to hire me whenever he needed something done.

BC: Did you feel that you could make a personal image out of these?

ERWITT: Absolutely not. Life was much simpler—you just took pictures of people, you used a couple and kept the rest. Generally it was done at the publisher's, in their library. Sometimes you'd go out with them, take a walk in the park and take a few snaps.

BC: *I read once that you used an auto horn to startle your subjects.*

ERWITT: No, that was much later. That's just to get people's attention. You use the horn when you are in a public situation. The horns help turn people in your direction.

JD: *What was it that got you interested in photography?*

ERWITT: I was interested in making a living in the least painful way I could figure out. It seemed like a good way because you could be your own person, your own boss, pick your own times.

JD: *What do you think of portraiture now?*

ERWITT: It's fine. I do everything. I don't care what it is. I don't like to do anything too often because it gets boring, but I like doing architecture a lot.

BC: *Have you ever turned down an assignment because it simply didn't appeal to you?*

ERWITT: Sure, or because I'm too busy. Generally I just like to keep busy. It doesn't matter what it is, as long as it's not tacky. I've worked for the Florida Orange Growers with Anita Bryant, would you believe, and if I can do that, I can do anything. It's a living.

JD: *There is always a distinction made between your personal work and your professional work. Has it affected you in any way now that your personal work is in demand?*

ERWITT: Of course it's very modest that sort of demand. It's very pleasant, but it's no way to make a living if that's what you're implying. It's not substantial enough yet.

JD: *The Museum of Modern Art has a fairly substantial collection of your work.*

ERWITT: But you don't make a living from that. I'm very lucky in that respect. I've never felt that working in the market place was demeaning in any way. I haven't done anything dishonest ... I don't think I have anyway. The two things are totally different. One is working for other people and the other is working for yourself. When you work for other people, you have to produce what they expect from you. When you're working for yourself you just do whatever you like. Different things, different problems. Sometimes I feel sorry that I don't have more time to take care of things that appeal to me more than others, but it's my choice.

BC: *Assignments must also provide you with many opportunities to come up with good personal work.*

ERWITT: That's a very important point. I very often take time off before, after, and sometimes during an assignment to do that.

JD: *Can you tell us something about how you first got to Magnum?*

ERWITT: I was in the army, stationed in France, and I went to the Magnum office in Paris, and met Robert Capa who seemed sympathetic, and he promised he would take me in the minute I got out of the army, which he did, or which Magnum did.

JD: *Did you have photographic duties in the army?*

ERWITT: Because of my qualifications I was assigned to be an aircraft gunner. Luckily the position was closed so I became a darkroom man. . . . I did take a few pictures, but the pictures you take in the army, you know, at least at that time were . . . if there was an accident somewhere you'd go out and take a picture of the bent fender, and if the general or a colonel came in for inspection, you'd take a picture of him inspecting.

JD: *Have you read anything about the controversy about Robert Capa's picture of the Spanish soldier being shot?*

ERWITT: Yeah. Something about that. What?

JD: *That he had staged the photograph. Was that possible?*

ERWITT: I don't believe it. I don't believe it and I think that if you look at Robert Capa's record over the years its inconceivable that he would do something so silly as that. Somebody, I think, wants to get a little notice by saying something provocative, so they say something like that. You have to look at a man's output, not one of his pictures, to make a judgment. It's inconceivable to me that someone with the kind of integrity that Capa had would do something like that. But I wasn't there so I wouldn't know.

BC: *Capa aside, how would you feel about a photograph being staged?*

ERWITT: I suppose it depends on what your intent was. I mean if it's an advertising photograph, for instance, perhaps that's the only way you can do it. I would say that if you can do it so it's believable, then maybe you're not so bad. I think the chances are that you wouldn't succeed.

JD: *Which photographers would you say have influenced you?*

ERWITT: Photographers? Just people in general, I mean artists in general, but if you go to photographers, I suppose Atget, Cartier-Bresson, and Kertesz. You know, the obvious people.

JD: *How do you approach an assignment like "Ten types typical of the American West"?*

ERWITT: How do I approach it? I rent a car and drive to the place and take the pictures. There's no great mystique. A lot of photographers like to put their hand to their forehead and tell you how they've suffered and so forth. It's really very simple, you know. If you're told what the problem is, you go out and do it. It's no big deal.

JD: *Your first exhibition at the Museum of Modern Art, "Improbable Photos," was in 1965. Do you enjoy having a museum as a showplace for your work?*

ERWITT: Well, that's the ultimate ego trip. Sure.

JD: *Do you prefer to have your images displayed on a wall as opposed to in a book?*

ERWITT: Either way. If it's your own personal work it makes no difference where it is. It could be in the men's room if it affects anyone.

JD : The scale doesn't mean anything to you?

ERWITT: Well, let's see. If it's at the Museum of Modern Art, it has a special meaning because that's the ultimate. Or the Smithsonian—the Smithsonian is not the ultimate place but it's very crowded. A lot of people see it, and that's very pleasant. Exhibits come down in a month, though. Books are permanent, and even though they're seen by fewer people they're good reference material. Each in its own way is rewarding. I like to have prints on the wall because you gain one generation.* Between print and book you lose this, that and the other thing. Then there are other problems—layout, for instance—whereas on the wall you just see the picture and it's not that important what's next to it or before it. It's sort of important but not terribly because you're more involved with the image. So I suppose the wall is the best place.

JD : Your prints are usually all around the same size, 11x14 or 16x20. Is there a reason for this?

ERWITT: It's convenient to print 11x14 or 16x20.

JD : In your personal work, there seems to be very little color. Do you prefer shooting in black-and-white?

ERWITT: I think color is OK for movies, which I do, and it's OK for working for people, but it's not OK for my personal work. It gives you information, but I don't like it. It's cumbersome. With black-and-white you have contacts, the negatives are put away, you can make prints and work on them yourself. Color you can't, you have to send it to somebody. There is also no way as of now that any color print will last in its original state for more than five years. Black-and-white can be as

*"Generation" refers to the closeness of the image to the photographer's negative. An original print from that negative is "first generation"; a print made by photographing the original print is "second generation."

permanent as anything. It's simpler, it's more abstract—when it's good.

JD : How much of your work goes on in the darkroom?

ERWITT: It depends on the print. I don't putz around too much if you're talking about solarization, or this and that.

JD : Cropping?

ERWITT: Usually not. I don't think when I'm taking pictures. I just take pictures. I just discovered a whole bunch of pictures that I'd taken a long time ago that I'd never even looked at, and I'd taken them about five, six, seven years ago, and there's all kinds of nice pictures in there and I don't remember taking them. I know they are my pictures though. When you're taking pictures you're taking pictures. You think for a second, and then it's gone.

JD : When you actually release the shutter, are you aware of the camera?

ERWITT: Sometimes, and sometimes you're fooled. Sometimes you think you've done terrific stuff and it's shit, sometimes you don't remember anything and it's terrific.

JD : John Szarkowski called the theory behind your photographs "The Indecisive Moment." How did that strike you?

ERWITT: He's a very funny fellow. I liked it a lot.

JD : The implicit comparison to Cartier-Bresson?

ERWITT: I'm flattered.

BC : It fits in perfectly with "anti-photographs." Could you talk about what an anti-photograph was? Or why at the time you called it an "anti-photograph"?

ERWITT: It seemed like a good idea at the time. A copywriter friend of mine, a very smart fellow, gave me that title and it seemed provocative, clever and so forth. I asked him why does it apply, and he told me, but I've forgotten.

JD : Is there any way in which your photography has been affected by being a member of Magnum? Is there some sort of collective force that is at work there?

ERWITT: No. Photography is a very individual thing. You don't take better pictures because you're a member of a group. It's affected an attitude toward the profession, but that's it.

JD : I understand your father is a Buddhist priest?

ERWITT: Something like that.

JD : Has that been any influence on you?

ERWITT LOOKS INCREDULOUS

JD : Quite seriously. When you look at someone like Minor White's work, he makes it quite clear that he's been influenced by Zen philosophy in his approach to photography.

ERWITT: In what way?

JD : In his theory of equivalence, and the way he sees the photograph as a symbol—one step in a dialogue between the viewer, his spirit, the photograph, and the image.

ERWITT: Oh Jesus Christ. Really? What crap. I tell you, he's a nice fellow I'm sure, and all that, but that kind of stuff makes me retch.

BC : Do you find yourself, when you're looking at other photographs, noticing how they've been done, professionally?

ERWITT: The kind of things that I personally react to are not the kind of things that make you wonder how they were done, because they're pretty straightforward. They're generally observations, and that's just a matter of seeing, not anything else. I react to content, primarily, and then there is also a kind of craft in prints. Prints can be terrific, but that's another level.

BC : And for you, that's not the most important level?

ERWITT: No. Quality doesn't mean deep blacks and whatever tonal range. That's not quality, that's a kind of quality. The pictures of Robert Frank might strike someone as being sloppy —the tone range isn't right and things like that—but they're far superior to the pictures of Ansel Adams with regard to quality, because the quality of Ansel Adams, if I may say so, is essentially the quality of a postcard. But the quality of Robert Frank is a quality that has something to do with what he's doing, what his mind is. It's not balancing out the sky to the sand and so forth. It's got to do with intention.

JD : You had some photographs in the Family of Man *exhibit. Was that a good showcase?*

ERWITT: It turned out to be OK, and no one imagined that that show would be so popular. I certainly didn't. In fact the show itself was OK, but I thought it was kind of sentimental and soupy. I mean it was nice, but I was staggered to see how popular it became. It must have hit a nerve somewhere. It was a good exhibit, but even more than that, it was so incredibly, brilliantly produced, exploited and advertised by the man who was master of it all, Steichen.

JD : Did you find that people's reactions were the same in Russia as America?

ERWITT: I remember the reaction in Russia. The Russians are always anxious to see anything, especially at that time, this was '59, anything that comes from the outside, they get so little of it. You can just pin up the pages of the New York phone book and you'll get a crowd.

JD : In your book Photographs and Anti-Photographs, *there seem to be a lot of photographs from the Iron Curtain countries. Do these countries hold a special fascination for you?*

ERWITT: I suppose. I spend time there, and I spend good time there. You don't go to Communist countries to do advertising photographs. You generally do editorial work, and out of that kind of work, good pictures come.

JD : Does the mood of the country affect the style of your photographs, your approach?

ERWITT: Well, I find that my best dogs are French dogs. But then again, French dogs have a special personality, so I don't know if it's the country. It's not a problem, it's just a matter of time. You can take good pictures anywhere. You can take good pictures in New Jersey.

JD : About your dog pictures, I noticed that one was taken as early as 1946, of a chihuahua in a sweater standing next to someone's shoes, and then in 1974 in the New York Times Sunday Magazine, *you did a fashion spread on shoes which was very much the same thing. How do you feel about doing something for that long?*

ERWITT: Actually my agent thought it would be a good idea for me to do something with dogs, because my dog book was coming out—to give it a little publicity.

BC : Did you ever see the movie Blow-up?

ERWITT: Yeah. It's OK. It had nothing to do with me.

BC : What do you think of the photographer in romantic imagination today?

ERWITT: It's OK because it keeps the prices up. I tell you, a lot of people get carried away with that aspect of it. The sad thing about it is that there is a craft involved, and it's amazing how many photographers or people who think they're photographers don't even know how to print or evaluate a print or know about optics. They don't know about the vocabulary but they sure know about Wynn Bullock.

JD : What do you think of photography coming into vogue and becoming commercially successful right now?

ERWITT: You mean *Vogue* magazine?

JD : There is a vogue and a demand for photography now—one example of this is the number of photography galleries springing up. Do you think it will educate people in any way to read photographs?

ERWITT: That's very narrow. As Szarkowski says, its getting more popular, but it's really an underground thing. I think it was bigger before when there were magazines and photographs were much more before the public. Now it's quite different, much smaller.

BC : Magazines like Look *and* Life *?*

ERWITT: Those were occasional showcases for some sort of photography, but what's in the galleries now is very narrow.

BC : Has the commercial publicity for photography brought us a larger number of good photographers, or do you think the good ones would have come anyway?

ERWITT: I think it's very sad that the magazines died, because they were the place that photographers could develop. I don't know if they can develop as well now. There are ten thousand photographers now and where are these people going to go?

BC : Would you say that you can tell right from the start whether a photographer is going to make it?

ERWITT: Definitely. I think you can tell right away because photography is not zone printing or any other nonsense like that. It's just seeing—at least the photography I care about. You either see or you don't see. The rest is academic. Anyone can learn how to develop, it's how you organize what you see into a picture. Perhaps you can develop it a little bit, but if you don't have the ability, learning the rest won't make you a good photographer. Photography, as I see it, is simply a function of noticing things, nothing more.

BC : Then your photography does not come out of a philosophy. It is entirely instinctive?

ERWITT: Totally. I mean my personal stuff.

JD : Do you think that the viewer should have any knowledge of some of the technical aspects of a photograph, or the conditions under which it was taken?

ERWITT: No. I think that just complicates things. I think you should just look at the stuff and if it enriches you in some way or knocks you out, that's all you need. I don't think it makes any difference. If you're a curious person, you'll find out something about it.

JD : What about the titling of a work? You usually title yours by place and date. Is that for any reason?

ERWITT: Some people like to describe their pictures but I think that's kind of stupid.

JD : What about the sequencing of pictures? Do you enjoy doing that?

ERWITT: You don't *do* them. You take pictures and then you look at your contacts and sometimes that's what you see. The only conscious one that I followed through on, that I knew what I was doing from the start, was somebody trying to close an umbrella. It was badly reproduced in *Photographs and Anti-Photographs*. In my beach book, which is the next one I'm working on, it will be properly reproduced. That sequence has to be seen clearly.

JD : Beaches and bitches—beaches are a favorite hunting ground of yours?

ERWITT: Beaches are terrific places to look for pictures. I'm just about finished shooting the pictures for a book whose working title is *Son of Beach*.

JD : What is it about beaches that particularly appeals to you? The great expanse to shoot against?

ERWITT: I think people who are half-naked are more interesting. All kinds of things come out of them on the beach. They are like pigeons there. It's a wonderful place.

JD : Do you find that if you're walking around without your camera and you see a good picture that you can't get, it ruins your day?

ERWITT: It's happened a few times.

JD : What do you think are the best qualities for a photographer to have?

ERWITT: A sense of independence. And it doesn't hurt to have independent means, because it's very difficult to make a living at it—increasingly difficult—and it's very hard to get recognition of any sort. Perseverance. To succeed at anything you need total dedication.

JD : Do you ever previsualize your personal photographs?

ERWITT: Never.

JD : Do you ever try to sneak your own personal attitude into your professional work?

ERWITT: Sure. Whenever it's possible.

JD : What satisfaction do you get from your professional work?

ERWITT: The fact that I make a reasonable living at it, the fact that you get published. It's very strange, you get professional work on the basis of your personal work, and you're allowed to do your personal work on the basis of your professional work.

JD : One photograph that was illustrated in the back of Photographs and Anti-Photographs *was the advertisement for Four Roses whiskey. Do you ever do an assignment like that and just get a satisfaction out of the fact that you've done a professional job as well as it can be done?*

ERWITT: I tell you, there's a big satisfaction involved in that particular picture. I got $5,000 for it. It was done in my house, in my studio, while I was listening to the hi-fi, and all the rest. It was a totally satisfying experience. It appeared all over as a huge ad., but if you're asking if it made my juices flow, no.

JD : Have you ever felt that your presence as a photographer has influenced the event?

ERWITT: Absolutely. Events have changed enormously from the time when I first started photographing. Now very often events

91

are set up for photographers. I don't mean just historical events, I mean even weddings. The weddings are orchestrated about the photographer taking the pictures, because, if it hasn't been photographed, it doesn't really exist. In that sense you influence an event.

BC : Do you personally find that events don't exist without photographs?

ERWITT: No, I think they exist with or without. But I know that once I was working on the year-end issue of *Life*—the love issue, if you remember it. It was my assignment to photograph weddings all over the country. I was appalled—they would have had the weddings on their heads if it was useful to your photography. I once had some people stand in a particular position that was more convenient for me so that when they released the rose petals at the end of the ceremony they all fell in the wrong place.

JD : You've made several films. What are the qualities that film has to offer over still photography?

ERWITT: The films I have done on my own have been documentary types. I'm interested in other things but I can't afford them because, you see, all the films that I've done, I've done on my own nickel. If I had had the money I would have done more ambitious things. But film is no joke, it's terribly expensive.

JD : What qualities do you think still photography has that motion pictures don't? What do you like in still photography?

ERWITT: I don't really make a connection. I think each thing has its own separate identity. The one unifying thing is the image. There are certain dynamics to visual things and that's true if you're talking of a block of ice, or serious pictures, or making movies. That aspect runs throughout. The problems are individual to the things that you're doing. It doesn't carry over. There are some still photographers I know who have become directors, but I haven't heard of photographers becoming cameramen. You see, the cameramen's union is still a bit closed, so no one can get in there until someone dies.

JD : Do you feel that the camera is innately honest?

ERWITT: I never give it a second thought. What do you mean by that?

JD: *Do you see the camera as being generous or cruel?*

ERWITT: Depends on what you do with it.

JD: *I mean innately.*

ERWITT: Innately it's nothing. The camera doesn't do it. It's the person behind it. You make certain decisions. I was never very fond of Mr. Nixon and I once went to the wedding of one of his daughters with the specific intention of taking unpleasant pictures of certain people I didn't like. The event was so spectacular, so well done, so beautiful, that I totally failed in my mission.

JD: *Do you believe in the power of photography to effect social change?*

ERWITT: Yes. Absolutely.

JD: *Does that affect a lot of your work?*

ERWITT: Not all. I'm sorry. I just don't. I don't like to get into this heavy attitude towards everything. I really don't have that.

JD: *When you're working as a photojournalist, for example when you took the picture of Jacqueline Kennedy at President Kennedy's funeral, do you ever have the feeling of being a* papparazzi, *intruding on people?*

ERWITT: I wasn't a *papparazzi* at all. I had a fixed position at the grave site that I think I must have won at a lottery.

BC: *Does a photographer need a thick skin to poke his camera into people's lives to get that crucial picture?*

ERWITT: Yeah, I think so. Not a thick skin so much, but sometimes you don't take pictures that you ought to because you don't want to offend somebody. I don't think that I have a particularly thick skin.

BC: *When you photographed Khrushchev and Nixon in the Kitchen Debate, did you feel that Nixon was playing to the camera?*

ERWITT: I don't think so in particular, but that whole trip was one of publicity and self-aggrandisement. I don't know if he was particularly conscious in that moment, but that whole trip was for the press, and the camera, and the television crew. It was ridiculous. Nixon was saying, "We're richer than you are"; and Khrushchev was saying, "We are catching up and will surpass you." That was the level of the debate.

BC: *Do you notice any trends developing in what's being done today in photography?*

ERWITT: It seems to me that photography with a big "P" is getting more artsy-craftsy and I think it's unfortunate. I don't know many photographers and I'm not terribly interested in them. I find them terribly serious in a very boring way. I don't like to be serious.

BC: *Do you think that photography is being exhausted, that people are struggling to come up with new stuff?*

ERWITT: Frankly I wouldn't know. I do know that I don't see very much stuff that interests me. My instinct tells me though that a lot of things that I'm interested in are just not happening. I get all sorts of magazines, and judging from what is in there, that stuff doesn't interest me at all. It's all sort of third-grade Ansel Adams. Ansel Adams doesn't interest me either, but it's that kind of thing. It's all very pretty, beautiful print quality, but I like the human comedy—that's the kind of thing I'm really interested in. What I'd like to see is people exploring emotional things, not sunsets. This kind of weird stuff, really I don't like.

JD: *Are there any of your own photographs that you particularly like?*

ERWITT: There's one that has particular poignancy for me at this time that I give to people when they either get married or divorced—which seems to be happening a lot these days. It's of the group in Bratsk getting married.

JD : Are there any other prints that you like?

ERWITT: The little dog jumping, and I like the crane and the faucet.

JD : The one of Hollywood in Photographs and Anti-Photographs *interests me because it seems quite different from the others. In most of your pictures the interest comes from a juxtaposition of images, but this one seems to rely on its strong composition.*

ERWITT: It has a meaning for me. I grew up there and it seems to be a fairly accurate picture of the place as I see it.

JD : As a photojournalist, which do you think are some of your more important pictures? The one of Jacqueline Kennedy is certainly one of the best-known.

ERWITT: It's important because it's a picture of Jackie Kennedy. Otherwise it's just a lady at a funeral. I tell you, if a picture can become an important picture because it's not Jackie Kennedy, because it's not Nixon and Khrushchev, because it's not any of those things, then it's worth something.

BC : What's the biggest mistake a photographer can make?

ERWITT: I must confess that I have a very narrow view of things. The failing that I see in most photographers is absolute serious-ness, which drives me up a tree. Photographers are really very pompous and very serious, generally speaking.

BC : Is it insecurity about themselves or their medium?

ERWITT: I just think a lot of people are serious. I just read something by one of my colleagues in the last issue of *Camera* that made me throw up. I mean, it sounds a little like Mr. White, except that he was a man of a certain age and has accomplished something so he can do that. He's done good work. But you get these idiots, these little kids that have done nothing and all of a sudden they're going off into all kinds of this stuff. Perhaps that's insecurity. You ought to hit them.

Minor White

WINDOWSILL DAYDREAMING *Rochester, New York, 1958*

Two Forms Moving Left and Right *Point Lobos, 1949*

Two Barns and Shadow *New York, 1955*

Imogen Cunningham

THE PLEA, *1910*

ALFRED STIEGLITZ, *1934*

BANANA PLANT, *1920's*

Cornell Capa

SIGNING UP MIGRANT LABOR *El Salvador, 1974*

BORIS PASTERNAK *Peredelkino, 1956*

BOLSHOI BALLET SCHOOL *Moscow, 1958*

Elliott Erwitt

From SON OF BITCH

From PHOTOGRAPHS AND ANTI-PHOTOGRAPHS

Yousuf Karsh

WINSTON CHURCHILL *"Here was the man who marshaled the English language and sent it into battle when we had little else."* EDWARD R. MURROW

ERNEST HEMINGWAY, 1957 *A man of peculiar gentleness—the shyest man I ever photographed.*

GEORGIA O'KEEFFE, 1956 *From the arid sparseness of her adobe home in New Mexico this noted American woman painter has chosen to eliminate anything which might interfere with her artist's vision.*

Arnold Newman

ALFRIED KRUPP, *Essen, Germany, 1963*

CLAES OLDENBURG, *1967–72*

IGOR STRAVINSKY, *New York City, 1946*

Lord Snowdon

ELIZABETH TAYLOR, *1971*

MENTAL HOSPITAL, *1968*

THE AMISH PEOPLE, A RELIGIOUS SECT IN PENNSYLVANIA, *1972*

ALEXANDER CALDER AND HIS WIFE IN SACHÉ, *1967*

Brett Weston

GLACIER LAKE, *1973*

Yousuf Karsh

Yousuf Karsh was born in Mardin, Armenia, in 1908. He emigrated to Canada as a young boy, and later went to work in Boston in the studio of the portrait photographer, John H. Garo.

In 1932 he returned to Canada and opened his own portrait studio in Ottawa. His cover pictures for *Life* magazine, most notably those of George Bernard Shaw, Winston Churchill and Ernest Hemingway, brought him international prominence as a photographer of the famous. His portraits, mostly taken with an 8x10 view camera, are known for their rich texture, extreme clarity, and dignified tone.

His exhibition "Men Who Make Our World" was featured in the Canadian Pavilion at Expo '67 and later toured the world. His books include *Faces of Destiny*, *Portraits of Greatness*, *This is the Mass*, *Karsh Portraits*, and *In Search of Greatness*, his autobiography.

When Yousuf Karsh first saw the tape recorder he shook his head. "No, I don't want to be recorded," he said. "You must take down what I say. I will speak very slowly. I have been misquoted, my words taken out of context too many times, I'm sorry."

This had never happened before. Nervously we explained that we would transcribe the tape, edit it, send it to him for his approval.

Nothing would be printed that he didn't want. He argued, we pleaded—an interview that would be at least two hours long, how could we write it all down and remain true to the interview as it happened? Finally he agreed.

It is not an easy thing to give an interview away from your home ground, and Yousuf Karsh was interviewed in a conference room in the Yale Club library in New York. Arriving at the club with his wife, Estrellita, he emerged from the revolving doors into the unfamiliar surroundings wearing a black coat, blazer, and a battered felt hat. A small and slender man, Karsh's personality comes out in his words, not his looks.

During the interview, Karsh remained quite formal. He sat erect, his hands clasped before him on the table. He speaks slowly and carefully in a manner that keeps you at a distance; and it is only by drawing oneself away from the sound that one begins to understand the meaning of the words. He is aware of his identity in relation both to his famous sitters and to the society that honors him for recording their images, and this complex role serves at times to obscure the artist and the man.

On the way out, I gave Karsh a quick tour of the club library, said to be the largest private library in America. As he took in the book-filled paneled walls and well-worn leather armchairs, he said to me: "I doubt that you would have elicited from me as much

99

as you did if we had not been in such beautiful surroundings."

JD: In In Search of Greatness *you tell of how, when you were young, you would find people on the street whose faces interested you and ask to photograph them. Do you still do this today?*

KARSH: The human face is a great challenge to me and I am very curious. Yes, when I see an arresting face, I invite him or her to be photographed. I still do all the spontaneous things I did as a young photographer, except adding to it the experience I have now.

JD: Do you find that people now recognize you on the street in Ottawa?

KARSH: They recognize me just as readily in New York, Paris and London; I travel eight and a half months a year.

To return to your first question, though, I find that even the unknown whom I invite to be photographed, to my delight, often turn out to be people who have had a very interesting life.

JD: So is there something in the physiognomy of the great that you instinctively pick out?

KARSH: Not always do the features of the great reveal their true character. In most cases I think you sense greatness. You sense goodness about people. This is not to say one is not apt to make significant mistakes in judgment—that's human nature —and we know from history that we often select a leader, and lo and behold, his record is black.

JD: To go back a bit, I understand you started doing portraiture with Garo.

KARSH: Yes. It was really a most marvelous experience for me, meeting this tremendously human and gifted artist. He used exclusively available light—not artificial light, but the glorious natural light of the northern sky.

From four o'clock on, as you know, the Boston weather is often unpredictable, so Garo decided to turn that part of the day into a social event. His friends would call on him and enjoy his liquid hospitality, and, as Garo's apprentice, I was the fortunate observer. More often than not, the conversation would be very stimulating and inspiring. One day it might be very frivolous, the next day it would be extremely serious, or the subject of music might come up. Garo had acquaintances in the worlds of art, letters, and science. So, for a young lad, although I did not have a great deal of academic training, this was like having a post-graduate course in the most impressionable years of one's life. It was a very beautiful experience for me. And only as recently as two weeks ago, I photographed one of the subjects who used to call on Garo, Arthur Fiedler, the conductor of the Boston Pops.

JD : How long were you in Boston for?

KARSH: For three years altogether, but I had to return to Canada every six months to renew my visa as a student entering the United States.

JD : Looking back on your time with Garo, do you see it as an apprenticeship?

KARSH: Yes, definitely, and it was the most important influence I had in my photographic career, since I was with Garo during my formative years.

JD : Where did you take your first photograph?

KARSH: In Canada. My uncle, George Nakash, who was a photographer, had given me a little Brownie camera. I took one of my photographs, enlarged it, and gave it to a schoolmate of mine as a little Christmas gift. Unbeknown to me, he entered it in a competition. To my surprise and delight, it won first prize! The award was fifty dollars in gold. To me, at that time, it was an enormous sum. I gave my friend ten dollars of it, and sent the other forty dollars to my family in Armenia. On such a nebulous happening, the beginning of a career is launched.

JD : How does the science of photography appeal to you as opposed to the art?

KARSH: The art is the challenge which you must meet every

day; the technique you should learn to control with time. The science and the art of photography are really one, and not opposed to each other.

JD: So you are not particularly inspired by the magic of the darkroom?

KARSH: The darkroom should be a logical extension of the photographer's eye. The darkroom is where the revelation of your photograph takes place. This unfolding is what fascinates me. My uncles were extremely gifted penmen and heraldic artists. Perhaps I inherited from them an artistic sense.

JD: With the work that you do today, how much is commissioned?

KARSH: My work has always mostly been by assignment. On the other hand, my curiosity is such that if, for example, I am in London and the person I am photographing is suddenly interrupted by a telephone call from Helsinki, at once it brings to mind Sibelius—and this happened. My London host made it possible for me to photograph Sibelius.

Similarly, when I photographed André Malraux, he said, "Thank you for having finished so promptly because I must go and receive Albert Schweitzer. I then photographed Schweitzer. André Malraux, however, was an assignment for *Life* magazine. Very often, too, I seek out, on my own, personalities I wish to photograph.

JD: Did you like having the magazines, especially Life, *as a showcase for your work because it reached so many people?*

KARSH: Not only that. Showcase is a good word because the format was so impressive. The quality of reproduction at that time was admirable and, of course, the magazine reached millions. The first time my photographs appeared in *Life*, they featured twenty-one pages of my work with my portrait of George Bernard Shaw on the cover. As a young photographer, this was very exciting for me. When President Kennedy was assassinated, *Life* used my photograph of him on the cover of their memorial issue. And when I brought back from Russia the first photographs made by a photographer—Eastern or Western—of Khrushchev and the members of the Soviet

Praesidium, a great many pages were devoted to these photographs. It was not unusual for people to frame photographs from *Life*. When I went to Russia, I was delighted to see my photograph of Hemingway on the walls of many of the intellectuals there.

JD: I read that at one point you were interested in going into medicine. Do you see any parallels between medicine and photography?

KARSH: I like to think that the trust engendered in a photographic sitting is akin to the trust one places in a compassionate doctor. Also, I strive for perfection. I like dedication. No physician can reach great heights without those qualities. But without having gone into medicine, I assure you that I have kept up my interest in it. Yesterday I photographed one of the foremost pathologists in the world, and seldom does a month pass by without my photographing a celebrated physician. I have just presented a collection of portraits of outstanding physicians called "Healers of our Age" to the Countway Library of Medicine (Harvard and Boston Medical Libraries) in Boston. It is by way of saying "thank you" for all that city has given me.

BC: Do you see the camera as a stethoscope? Does it engage you in life more closely?

KARSH: Not consciously. I presume my experience acts in that manner because, when I photograph someone, I like to feel, as Cecil B. DeMille once told me, that I "photograph people's thoughts."

Sometimes, as a portrait photographer, my subjects tell me intimate things they want you to know, assuming that it is important for your recording an interpretation of their character.

MRS. KARSH: As I have noticed Yousuf with various people, I do make the definite parallel between the medical consultation and the intimate photographic session—especially the way Yousuf approaches it, in the sense that he establishes rapport with the subject.

KARSH: But that comes naturally.

MRS. KARSH: So does the intuition of a great diagnostician.

KARSH: I think that the subject's trust comes first. It is not exactly the same approach as a physician would use because the person is there to be diagnosed. In the photographic session, I try to portray the consummation of all his experiences—and what the person, himself, represents.

JD : Do you think that the people who come to see you come, in one sense, to see who they are?

KARSH: No, I don't think so. All the people who come to see me have arrived. They may get reassurance, or a shock, but they know who they are.

BC : People are often surprised to see what they look like.

KARSH: I think it's very destructive for the photographer to involve himself with any self-image the sitter may have, for it clouds his own perception. Yes, it is true—people are surprised to see what they look like. For many people, it is as much a surprise to encounter their image, as hearing their voice for the first time over a tape recorder. But, as for the photographer, at least for me, I give the best of my attention, of my dedication, to each situation.

JD : One reads of primitive people who are afraid to have their picture taken because they feel the camera can take some of their soul. Do you ever instinctively understand why some people get this feeling?

KARSH: I try to photograph people's spirit and thoughts. As to the soul-taking by the photographer, I don't feel I take away, but rather that the sitter and I give to each other. It becomes an act of mutual participation.

JD : You said that a good portrait is always a collaboration. Are there times, though, when the power balance is not so equal?

KARSH: I don't think of the photographic session in terms of power balance. I try to be as objective as I can when I photograph people.

BC : Do you also think in terms of a historical point of view—of recording an image that will stand up under time?

KARSH: Shouldn't any creative person do this? It is there regardless of whether you do it consciously or not. How can you possibly photograph an Einstein or a Helen Keller, or Eleanor Roosevelt, a Hemingway or a Churchill, and not realize they are already part of history? If your photograph is the summation of these people's many accomplishments, besides showing their human side, then the historical point of view is fulfilled.

JD : In the collaboration between the photographer and the sitter, what do you think is the most important quality that the sitter can bring? Honesty?

KARSH: I think if there is mental rapport between us, then honesty follows as a matter of course.

JD : You are often referred to as "Karsh of Ottawa," like a title. How did that come about?

KARSH: Well, David Low made a cartoon of me, and he said, "It is not a knighthood, but it should be." A Canadian cannot accept titles. But I settled in Ottawa, again the result of Garo's influence. I wanted to be in a city which would be a crossroads of the world. I had my unique happiness as a result of having settled in Ottawa. There I photographed Churchill, I photographed de Gaulle, I photographed a score of people just because I happened to be in a place where significant people have visited.

JD : There's a famous story behind that picture of Churchill.

KARSH: Yes, that was really a turning point in my career. But I would like to play down that little story that you have on your mind—about my removing the cigar from Churchill's mouth—because almost all reporters and journalists tell it better than I do. But certainly Churchill is one of the most popular photographs in the history of photography. Seven countries have used it for stamps.

JD : You have spoken a lot about the feeling of rapport between the sitter and the photographer. Do good photographs nearly always result from such feelings?

KARSH: Yes, of course. One of my favorite photographs is that of Georgia O'Keeffe. It almost symbolizes her whole life in this single photograph; there was understanding between us. If there is mental understanding, the rest comes naturally.

JD : In a historical context, your portraits deal with great people largely in the sense of good, but had the opportunity arisen, would you have wanted to photograph a Hitler or a Mussolini?

KARSH: Yes, indeed; I'm not a judge, I'm a recorder. If I had had the opportunity, I would have. I tried in vain to photograph Stalin. I would wish to record anyone of historical significance. I feel I would like to be as objective as possible, to let the photograph speak for history.

JD : Are you conscious with your photographs that some of them will become the definitive visual image of that person?

KARSH: I cannot deny that it happens. Winston Churchill, Albert Einstein, Eleanor Roosevelt, Helen Keller, Albert Schweitzer—they have become part of the history books. It's comforting, but I like to forget what I have done yesterday and go on with new challenges.

JD : I understand that you have your camera painted white. There must have been some purpose behind that though.

KARSH: Early in my career a little child commented, "Why is your camera black?" "Why black, indeed!" I thought. It is such a mournful color. So, for a short while my camera *was* white. It was during that period that this fact received a great deal of publicity.

BC : Do you find a common denominator in great painting, great literature, great music?

KARSH: Yes, and I think it affects us all our lives. When young people send me portfolios for suggestions and criticisms to help them, I always make it a point to say: be a student of the humanities, because if you are, it makes you a more sensitive recorder of life.

JD : Could we talk for a while about what goes on in the case of an individual portrait, how you go about doing it? Is there a favorite of yours that we can talk about?

KARSH: Yes. We've talked about the rapport, the meeting of minds, the preparation and the dedication, the involvement of the photographer and the objectivity of his approach. But there are times I find when you may prepare yourself too much.

For the most part, I find that preparation is useful only to help you familiarize yourself with the life and accomplishments of the subject. Beyond that it is not necessary, because these people are accustomed to giving so much of themselves. With any significant person, a philosopher, or a historian, you don't really need to burden yourself with much homework. If you like them, and they like you, the rest suggests itself.

I recall how interested I was to photograph Hemingway. A good friend of his tried to prepare me for the occasion and he said, "Now, all I would advise you to do, Karsh, is to learn to appreciate and drink Hemingway's favorite cocktail." Well, that was not a hardship. I asked what it was, and he said, "Daiquiri." So, when the sitting was arranged, both the Canadian and American ambassadors in Havana took me to meet Hemingway early in the morning. When they left, Hemingway went into the kitchen and called out to me, "Karsh, what would you like to drink?"

"Daiquiri, sir," I shouted back.

"Good God," he said, "at this time of day!"

BC : What is the actual process that you use to set up a portrait? The more technical steps.

KARSH: For many years I have photographed people in their own environment, so I carry my lights with me. The technical side is one phase I do not like to emphasize because memorable photographs have been made by the simplest of cameras using available light. I have a variety of cameras, from 35mm to the 8x10. My preference, still, because of my early discipline and training, are the larger formats. And when we take this beautiful 8x10 negative and blow it up to a large size, it is a great aesthetic experience. Still, I judge a photograph only by the final result. Had my early training been with 35mm it would have made my whole life easier!

As recently as a few weeks ago, Dr. Edwin Land invited me to go to Cambridge, Massachusetts, for a surprise. When I got there, I was introduced to a 20x24 camera to accommodate 20x24 sheets of Polaroid film. In these days of transistorization, especially, it was impressively large. The size of the bellows, alone, hearkened back to Mathew Brady days. When the 20x24 Polaroid print was peeled off, the color resolution and the quality of the color were so subtle that everyone applauded. So do not be surprised to see me travel all over the world with both 35mm and the 20x24 camera!

JD : How often do you take portraits in color?

KARSH: Almost always. I repeat everything in color and black-and-white.

BC : Do you ever use makeup on your subjects?

KARSH: No, definitely never! I never apply makeup. Women, of course, come in already made up. I think you are asking this question because you have seen some editions of my books where the beautiful, yet unpredictable, process of sheet-fed gravure was so contrasty that it exaggerated the highlights on the face. This certainly was not the case in my first major book, *Portraits of Greatness,* and will not be so in my forthcoming book, *Karsh Portraits.*

JD : Can we talk a little about posing? You have been criticized for a sometimes artificial use of hands.

KARSH: Basically I see a picture all complete with the hands an integral part of the subject—not unrelated. If you look at my photographs—Shaw, for example, you will have a little more understanding of this Irish giant, his bearing, and his attitude, of which the hands are so expressive, yet subordinate to the strong intellectual face.

JD : As a portrait photographer, your one great tool is obviously light. How long did it take you to reach a satisfactory knowledge of how to use it, to come to grips with some of the possibilities?

KARSH: As you know, during my training with Garo I worked only by available light. It was not until my early days in Ottawa that I became aware of the possibilities of what is now called artificial light. But working with light remains for me elusive and constantly challenging. I don't think I will ever conquer the mystery of light.

BC: You have photographed some people in their environment, such as Georgia O'Keeffe, and then you have photographed other people closer up. Is this because with certain faces you are more interested in the sculptural aspects?

KARSH: At the time of making the photograph, I did not think consciously about aesthetics, only what seemed right at that particular moment for that particular subject.

BC: Do you think that there is such a thing as a complete portrait, one photograph that can show the essence of a wide-ranging personality?

KARSH: Yes, I have been told my Churchill is one example. This is the very thing I strive for. I don't always succeed but that's the aim. It's the hope of every photographer.

BC: What is a likeness?

KARSH: If it's a likeness, alone, it's not a success. If, through my portraits, you can come to know the subject more meaningfully, if it synthesizes your feelings toward someone whose work has imprinted itself on your mind—if you see a photograph and say, "Yes, this *is* the person" with a little new insight—that is a beautiful experience.

JD: In your book Portraits of Greatness *there is a page of text next to every photograph. How do you see the printed word in relation to photography?*

KARSH: I don't believe that words are needed to explain a photograph; a photograph explains itself. But I have had the

109

unique experience of photographing many of the gifted men and women of our time. The reason there is a written profile with each photograph is that I would like to share my rich experience with the reader.

JD : Inevitably we come to the question of how you came to photograph the famous.

KARSH: I think it was the influence of Garo. He introduced me to gifted men and women. Incidentally, up to the time I photographed Winston Churchill, I used to photograph 99 percent women. With Garo, I witnessed what a wonderful conversationalist and host he was. People from the world of opera, the arts and letters, would come to his studio. I would see them as human beings, as well as artists at the pinnacle of their careers. I realized there was something more than just a God-given voice, in the case of an opera star. That person had discipline and had studied his or her art. An architect would call on Garo and tell of the magic he aspired to build. He compared his building with the ancient construction of Babylonian days. This is all in retrospect, of course. At the time I just admired them as individuals. They inspired me, and I hoped I could continue to be in surroundings where I would meet more of such people. Today, for me, the wonderful thing is to meet and know the younger would-be giants.

JD : You once said, "I am satisfied that no purpose would be served if I were to convert consciously what should be a portrait of greatness into a moment of weakness." Was this an attack of the hyper-realistic genre of portraiture?

KARSH: This was not an attack on any genre, but a statement of my own beliefs. I know it would be more sensational if I were to photograph a famous person doing something ridiculous, but this is not my personal inclination. I do have reverence and respect and I appreciate people. The aesthetic still has high priority with me. There would be no difficulty in making any human being look demented. On the other hand, I would be equally unfair to the subject if I tried to make all of them look saintly. I try very hard not to interpose any of my own bias. I try to be objective. This is the most difficult thing in the world.

JD : Are there any photographers, apart from Garo, who were a great influence on you?

KARSH: Steichen showed me great friendship late in his life, and I was imbued with his philosophy.

JD : When you photographed him, did you discuss photography?

KARSH: No, not exclusively. He was interested in many things. My earlier photographs of Steichen were when he was a Commander in the navy in the Second World War. Later I photographed him at his home, and he returned the compliment and photographed my wife and me when he was quite old, and had stopped taking photographs.

BC : Would you ever be able to do that, stop taking pictures?

KARSH: No, I would not. I would always want to have that curiosity of traveling all over the world, meeting people in their own environment. I do not basically believe in retirement; there is no reason for it.

JD : What do you think about the effect the art market is having on photography today? The destroying of negatives, for example, to make limited editions.

KARSH: I was offered a tremendous fortune to destroy one or more of my negatives. I don't think negatives should be destroyed.

JD : Is there any advice that you would give to a young photographer today?

KARSH: Again, I don't believe in using the camera without first enriching your life in the humanities. When you do that, and when you master how to operate a camera, the camera becomes a tool, just as a pen is to a writer. He doesn't think about the formation of each letter, and the use of the camera should also become second nature. I would tell a young photographer today to be a student of the humanities, to be able to think, to be able to observe, to take advantage of what you see around you—you should do that before you click the camera.

Arnold Newman

Arnold Newman was born in New York in 1918. He studied art at the University of Miami, originally wanting to become a painter, but in 1939 he began work in photography, moving to Philadelphia to become an apprentice to Leon Perskie, a professional photographer and friend of his family's. At Perskie's studio, Newman had to photograph up to seventy subjects a day, and he soon began photographing independently.

On a trip to New York in 1941, Newman met Beaumont Newhall, director of the photography department of the Museum of Modern Art, who suggested that he show his work to Alfred Stieglitz. Stieglitz was encouraging and later that year, Newman had a joint exhibition with Ben Rose at the A.D. Gallery.

Moving to New York, Newman opened his own studio, concentrating on portraiture. He became acquainted with the New York painters and sculptors of the time and they became his most interesting subjects. In 1945 the Philadelphia Museum of Art held a one-man exhibit of his portraits of artists titled "Artists Look Like This." It was purchased by the museum and widely circulated.

Since then, Newman has photographed five United States presidents, nearly every contemporary artist of note, writers, actors, musicians, and world leaders. His work has appeared in

every major picture magazine as well as in exhibitions throughout America. *One Mind's Eye*, his first book, containing over 150 portraits, was published in 1974.

The number of Arnold Newman's photographs that have come to be known as definitive portraits is staggering. Stravinsky, Picasso, Kennedy, Mondrian, are only a few. Taken together, the portraits are an unparalleled documentation of twentieth-century genius. We interviewed the man who took these photographs at his apartment off Central Park West, arriving mid-morning on a Sunday. Ushering us in, his first words were, "I hope you haven't eaten yet."

Arnold Newman is a robust man with a Vandyke beard and black horn-rimmed glasses. On the day we interviewed him he was dressed in a sport shirt and slacks. During the brunch of lox, bagels, and herring that Mrs. Newman had fixed, food was a more pressing issue than photography. We did find out, however, that Newman met his wife, Augusta, twenty-nine years ago when she was helping Teddy Kollek run guns to Israel for the Haganah.

The taped interview lasted for over three hours and was conducted in the living room of Newman's apartment and later in his studio. The apartments in the Newmans' building were originally built as artist's studios and the living room of Newman's duplex was as open as a small airplane hangar. The walls were covered with African art, Newman photographs, and several pieces of modern art from his own collection, many of which Newman has acquired by swapping photographs for work by his sitters. There were two small Mondrian drawings, a Claes Oldenburg painting on plexiglass, a Raphael Soyer, a deKooning, several Giacomettis, as well as a score of other modern masters. A small study of a dancer, one of Newman's own drawings, hung inconspicuously in the dining room.

Scattered among the famous Newman portraits were several snapshots of the Newmans at what at first look like family dinner parties. On closer inspection, the guests turn out to be Man Ray, Marcel Duchamp, Igor Stravinsky, Marilyn Monroe, and Carl Sandburg.

After the interview, Newman led us out to see his studio, four doors down the street in what had actually been his first combination darkroom-apartment. "Now I commute," he chuckled.

He gave us a complete tour of his work area, pointing out the extensive filing system he uses to store his negatives, prints, and records of magazine assignments. In another room his wife was making last-minute arrangements for an assignment that would take them to Europe the next day. As we poked around, Newman amused us with stories of a professional photographer's life. Once he had been sent to Italy to shoot a wine advertisement and had arrived to find that the dark grapes were out of season. Under a deadline, he ended up buying a bunch of green grapes imported from Israel and spray-painting them purple.

In the large studio workroom, three steel boxes, a dozen forty-foot electrical cords, three floodlights, and fifty boxes of film sat next to his camera case waiting for inspection before departure. "I could tell you about the time the airlines lost my cameras for three days," said Newman, gesturing with one of the cigars that seem as much a part of his shooting equipment as his cameras, "but I won't."

BC: *I know it's a blunt question, but can you say why you do portraits?*

NEWMAN: Because I have to and love to. I began taking portraits because I had some visual ideas that I wanted to express, and I was and still am fascinated by people and what makes them tick.

What are people really like? We're all curious about other human beings because they are the most complex and fascinating things in the world. Other people find nature or the movements of the universe exciting, but for me it is the personality of individuals and the worlds they create.

BC : Is this because you want to find something out about yourself?

NEWMAN: We all measure ourselves every day by other human beings, by everyone we meet. I'm interested in people who do things and the hardest-working people I know are creative people: artists, musicians, writers. The motivation of these people and even the drive of the top business executive is exciting to me. I love to interpret people in a way that combines the graphic aspects of art that have always fascinated me, for instance design—design that relates to my feeling about these people and their work. Design is composition—anything that makes the picture work whether it is free or rigid in feeling. It all depends on what you have to say about that specific person. It is all related.

BC : Beaumont Newhall said that your more effective portraits seem almost self-portraits, "as if the sitter himself had conceived the image." How do you respond to this?

LAUGHTER FROM NEWMAN

NEWMAN: Originally we all see through and are influenced by the minds and visions of others. I remember driving through the south of France for the first time and the Arles landscape was straight out of Van Gogh; Aix-en-Provence was pure Cézanne; and when I stepped out on the balcony of our hotel at Nice, all I could see was Matisse. As it turned out, Matisse had actually lived there and painted from those same balconies. Other people's ideas influence our lives daily, if only for a brief moment, so my portraits are a reflection of them. The people I photograph are self-portraits only in the sense that I am relating to them with something specific in mind. This is what Beaumont meant. If my photographs don't tell you something about these people, then they are not good portraits. *This is of great importance*: A good portrait must first be a good photograph. It isn't enough just to make a pleasing image. When my photographs work, they are successful because of the interpretation I have added to the straight portrait. The portrait has to be particular to that individual, whether it is reality or symbolism. The Stravinsky portrait, for example, was entirely symbolic. It isn't real at all, but it is particular to him. I try to make people become what they are when I photograph them.

If I photographed either one of you. . . . Hold it! Now look at the way you are both sitting. It's beautiful. If I were to photograph you this way someone might say, "He posed them. Nobody puts their hand up to their temple like that—it's artificial, a cliché." But people do that with their hands all the time. It is only a cliché because certain people have made it one. The pose has become stylized and unreal. But there is nothing wrong with being unreal unless you take an unreal situation and try to say that it is reality. Then it becomes wrong. There are many examples of this. So many people use artificial lighting and stylized poses and insist that we accept the images as real situations. We cannot believe them. However, there are many great photographers like Irving Penn and Richard Avedon who make photographs in a very unreal manner, but they ask you to accept their work on that level. Penn created a deliberately different and artificial voice, like a poet does to interpret his world. He doesn't say, "This is completely real." He combines the real with the unreal.

We can believe in the reality of fantasy, but to create fantasy and ask us to accept it as unconditionally real because it came out of a camera is unacceptable. I do not ask you to believe that my portrait of Stravinsky is real in the sense of a pure record photograph. It is a symbolic portrait, not reality, and I ask you to accept it on that level.

JD : How much photography do you do in your studio?

NEWMAN: As little as possible. For me the studio is a sterile world that only becomes interesting when my background panels become worn and tattered—become real!

There are times, of course, when for practical reasons I have no choice but to work in the studio; then I accept the artificiality of it and proceed from there, and I must admit that I like some of the results. But for me the changing world outside is the most exciting.

BC : Could we go back to the beginning of your photographic career?

NEWMAN: I've been trying to get away from it. What aspect?

BC : How you first got involved.

NEWMAN: I started off intending to be nothing but a painter. I had a certain amount of talent and it's hard to say where it would have led if I had continued with it. I might have become a first-rate painter, or merely a good third-rate painter. I grew up in the Great Depression and was lucky to have parents who would even consider giving me art lessons. In our house books, art, and music were enjoyed and respected—your typical, good middle-class Jewish background. My parents encouraged my art.

I joined the Boy Scouts at age twelve and met Ben Rose, one of the important photographers working today, and what is so strange and wonderful is that our careers and personal lives have paralleled right up to recently when the French magazine *Photo* did big articles on Ben and me back-to-back. That's forty-six years. We had our first New York show together in 1941 at the A.D. Gallery. About that time Ben had the cover and I had a portrait in an issue of *Harper's Bazaar*. I learned a great deal from Ben. You learn as much from fellow students as you do from teachers and Ben really opened up my eyes to photography. We and our wives are still close friends.

BC : You started out as a painter and ended up as a photographer. How do you explain this conversion?

NEWMAN: In the summer of '39 I found that despite a job and a working scholarship, I was financially unable to return to art school. One day when I was walking down the boardwalk in Atlantic City (my hometown) trying to figure out what I was going to do, I ran into a friend of my father who offered me a job to learn photography in his portrait studio in Philadelphia. My father suggested I could always make a living at it and I figured that I would work at photography during the daytime and study art at night. One night during my first days there, I went with Ben and a group of friends to take pictures on Dock St, of Philadelphia. I was so excited by what they were doing that I decided to give up painting temporarily. I never went back. It got so that I would stay in my boss's darkroom until two in the morning printing my own work and I began shooting lunch hours and weekends. Underpaid. I somehow managed to keep myself going by borrowing a dollar or two from Ben. Looking back on it, I'm convinced that if I had been walking the other way on the boardwalk at Atlantic City, that I'd be a painter today. People say they have control over the direction of their lives, but only to a certain degree.

But when you say conversion: How different is photography from painting? How different is painting from sculpture, or print-making from drawing? It is interrelated. I think that my emotional makeup enabled me to be very good at it.

BC: I understand that when you were painting you were very influenced by the realist school.

NEWMAN: At first, yes. I had been observing and absorbing images all my life. At that time there were very few abstract painters to look at that would influence our vision the way they do today. While still in high school, I remember being very anti-abstraction until Ben Rose helped me understand them. I had been isolated and hadn't really been able to figure out what these artists were trying to do. But once the "windows" were opened, it was exciting and I learned a great deal just by looking.

Cubism and modern painting then became a strong influence on my vision of art and photography. The delicately worked out composition was very much in my mind. On the other hand, my earlier photographic work was more realistic and emotional. We all begin somewhere: early Beethoven was Mozart, early Picasso was Lautrec. Nobody comes full-blown. I was influenced by the photographs of the Farm Security Administration, particularly by Walker Evans; some of my early work was pure Walker Evans. We can't help but be influenced by what came before us. It's a normal learning process.

BC: What are the basic differences between seeing as a photographer and as a painter?

NEWMAN: The ability to understand and differentiate between

reality and a completely made-up world, and, of course, to be able to present your own vision. You have to have a good technical sense to be a good photographer, but I have a feeling that a good painter will always be a good photographer if he sets his mind to learning the techniques, which are really as easy as driving a car.

There has been a great deal written about the influences of painting on photography. I feel they are very much alike. They originate from the same sources. Look at the photographs by painters like Charles Sheeler, Reginald Marsh, Kuniyoshi, and Degas. Degas struggled with photography because he had the image in the back of his mind but the technique hadn't been invented. He would have been a great 35mm photographer, though I can hear a lot of painters saying, "Thank God they didn't give him a 35mm!" Great artists have always understood, appreciated, and allied themselves with photography long before the general public did. The Impressionists for example. American painters like Thomas Eakins and Ben Shahn used photographs mostly for studies for their paintings, but many of the photographs themselves were marvelous works of art. Both Daguerre and Muybridge were second-rate painters whose real achievements were made in technical photography. This is not to say that to be a good photographer you have to be trained as a painter, but it seems to help.

BC: You once said that the difference between painting and photography was that painting was creative distortion and photography was creative selection.

NEWMAN: Like a lot of quotes, that's an oversimplification, but basically it is true. A painter can do anything he wants: he can distort line and color or not even bother with real images, that is, images directly representing what he sees before him. A photographer must deal with the reality of what is in front of his camera. As long as he says, "I have changed this reality," then it is acceptable. If you can see that something has been changed by hand, by mixed media or collage, or that something has been torn—it is all right as long as you don't try to say, "This is real," like Rejlander or Robinson did.* The composite

*Oscar Gustav Rejlander and Henry Peach Robinson were two selfconsciously "artistic" photographers of the mid- and late-nineteenth century. Both made photographs in which a single print was printed from a number of negatives.

works by these men were done with the intention of having the viewer accept them as real photographs, not faked and put together. For example, commercial portraiture sometimes misuses the technique of vignetting which originally is a very real way of seeing things. There's nothing wrong with using vignetting as long as it is being used to make a photographic statement and not to imitate etching or painting. Tearing a photograph in half may bother you but it is a statement. You can then say, "I have torn this, I have changed this, I have made a statement." It seems perfectly all right when Larry Rivers or Robert Rauschenberg combine photographs with paint, so why should it be wrong for a photographer to do that?

The power of photography lies with the power of the undeniable reality of the image. When you physically change a photograph, you change the source of that power. But it is acceptable providing that the viewer is made aware of this manipulation. Even my Warhol collage retains conviction because its basic source is undeniably photographic.

BC: Then the power of photography is not simply confined to realism, but can gain a new power when it is released from realism, as long as the artist or viewer is aware that this has been done? That it is not attempting to say something is real?

NEWMAN: It has freedom when the photographer can make a statement with his images, when he can say, "This is what I am." Then what is real? What is real about the medium of photography? Photography is very unreal. You take a three-dimensional world and reduce it to a two-dimensional world. You take color and reduce it to black-and-white. You take the world and life constantly moving within time, and reduce it to an instant moment. That's not real. It is an illusion of reality. There are many things that are very false about photography when it is accepted without question. You must recognize this and interpret it as you would any other art form, and then maybe it is a little more than real.

BC: You said that early in your career you had an idea about portraiture that could not be expressed in words and that only afterwards were you able to explain it intellectually.

NEWMAN: In a sense, yes. As a young photographer I did a lot of thinking and kept a notebook where I put down a few of my earth-shaking ideas. But sometimes these ideas couldn't be put into words even in retrospect. I was searching for certain kinds of visual ideas. In the beginning you don't think of it as art, you think of just trying to work something out. I was excited by what I saw, I was curious about what I didn't see, and I set out to fulfill some unexpressed ideas about portraiture.

My idea of photography came from the snapshot. As a boy I remember seeing a photograph of Teddy Roosevelt in a biography of him. In the official frontispiece portrait of the President, he looked like an embalmed, overstuffed walrus. But in another, a snapshot, he was photographed with his foot on top of a rhino or some other animal he'd shot and was grinning like mad and one could sense from a photograph like this one what the man really looked like, how he stood, even what he was like as a human being. I began to develop an idea that combined the reality of the snapshot with a creative graphic approach. I wanted to show where a person lived, where he worked, a kind of reality combined with a carefully worked out composition. I didn't set out to do something different so much as to do something that interested me. I wasn't trying to be avant-garde—that's being fashionable. You don't set out to revolutionize art, you make statements for yourself.

BC : Have you ever tried to explain the creative urge in yourself?

NEWMAN: I have a favorite story to explain that: in his auto-biography, Jean Renoir tells a story about his father, the painter, talking about Mozart, whom he worshipped: "He wrote music because he could not prevent himself. It was like having to pee." He considered the mode of expression unimportant. "If Mozart had not made music, he would have written poems or planted gardens." In any case, circumstance and necessity—in a word, the Depression—forced me to give up painting for photography.

If I wasn't in the field of art, I'd want to be an analyst because to me the human mind is the most fascinating thing in the world. What makes one person one thing and another person something else? These questions intrigue me.

BC : So you might see the photographer as an amateur psychologist.

NEWMAN: Not as an amateur psychologist but as a first-rate

artist. An artist has an insight that is very special. Different artists set out to create a work of art for different reasons. Some are primarily interested in expressing ideas within a medium. Others are more interested in their subject matter. I am interested in the combination of the two. I've been asked if my photograph of Stravinsky would have been significant or powerful if the man in the photograph had actually been the corner grocer instead of a musical genius. If that were the case, the photograph would merely have been a good design instead of a good portrait. The fact that it *is* Stravinsky made that picture.

The same is true for the portrait of Alfried Krupp. I was able to control this horrible human being and show him as he was essentially—the devil. The identity of the sitter is very important to me.

BC : Was the Krupp picture a deliberate hatchet-job?

NEWMAN: Absolutely deliberate. Here was a man who chained slaves to the machinery of his arms factory so they wouldn't run away when the bombers came (they weren't all Jews, I might add). Here was a man who underfed his workers even according to the Nazi standards so that when they were too weak to work he would ship them back to the concentration camps to be exterminated.

I set out to do whatever I could to him and was more successful than I hoped. I have always felt that if that one picture became my best-known, I could feel I had been a success as a photographer.

BC : So in many ways you see yourself going beyond conventional documentary biography?

NEWMAN: That *is* biography! What is biography—telling the story of a man who is pleasant and nice and kisses little children? Hitler kissed little children and slaughtered millions of others. What the hell is biography? What are human beings about?

And what is a photographer? Must he only be a twentieth-rate guy making snapshots at weddings so everybody looks pretty? There are very few Cartier-Bressons, Brassaïs and W. Eugene Smiths in the world, but to me, these men are *photographers*. They are artists because they make statements that all of us wish we could have made.

BC: How would you explain the interest most people have in photographs of famous artists, statesmen, or writers? We have their accomplishments, why do we need more?

NEWMAN: We simply want to know what they look like. We are fascinated by people who shape our lives, even if they shape them in a small way. Granted, you can't find out everything about a human being from one image. You'd need a movie fifty, sixty, seventy years long to show everything. The images that I make are only one out of millions possible. I try to make my portraits the common denominator of that person *at that time.*

I might add, though, that I'm not just interested in famous people. I just got finished photographing a cross-section of "ordinary people" in America for the "Face to Face" exhibit. These are people we see thousands of every day, but each one is in himself "everybody," and therefore fascinating as hell.

JD: In what perspective do you put the expressive nature of photography as opposed to the scientific nature?

NEWMAN: It's all part of the whole, like a three-legged stool. You kick out one leg and the whole collapses. In other words: Visual ideas combined with technology combined with personal interpretation equals photography. Each must hold its own; if it doesn't, the thing collapses.

BC: So you see a correlation between technological innovation and the growth of certain photographic movements?

NEWMAN: Very much so, starting right at the beginning with Daguerre and Talbot. I remember when my black-and-white film was either ASA 24 or 32 and we thought that was pretty fast. We were limited by our equipment, but the creative photographers kept trying to push it. I know many photographers who are not chemists or physicists who have pushed color and black-and-white photography way beyond its "limits" simply by trial and error. I'm often called a great technician but I know nothing about chemistry really; I've just learned something about photographic chemicals by experimenting. It seems a pity to me that many of the recent graduates from photography school don't know a damn thing about chemicals and their possibilities.

JD : In relation to other artists, isn't the photographer faced with, for lack of a better phrase, "unique limitations" by the science involved?

NEWMAN: Very much so, but it is just these limitations which make the medium so powerful.

BC : Could you talk about your choice of cameras?

NEWMAN: Basically I work with view cameras, 4x5 mostly. I thought for a long time that the 35mm wasn't my way of seeing. I learned with a view camera. The 35mm only seemed to add grain and lack detail. But when the single lens reflex came out, it was like a more portable and freer view camera, so I began using it. You are definitely influenced by the camera you use and have to adjust your vision to the instrument.

BC : At what age did you get your first camera?

NEWMAN: When I moved in with Ben Rose in Philadelphia, I borrowed a camera from an uncle of mine. It was a little folding view camera, a $2\frac{1}{4}$x$3\frac{1}{4}$ Contessa Nettle. I went right out to take pictures and a print from that very first day of photographing appears as the first photograph in my book *One Mind's Eye*. It was of a mother nursing a child. I was twenty years old and already had a vision of what I wanted to do because I had been watching other people doing this for a while and had time to think about it.

BC : What is your procedure for making a portrait?

NEWMAN: Well, it's like a businessman who gets up in the morning and if he doesn't find his name in the obituary column, he goes to work. I just decide I'm going to photograph someone and I go to it. I don't have any magic formulas, I just ask myself a few questions, do a lot of research on my sitters beforehand, and then ask them a few questions. People ask if I pose my

sitters. Yes and no. I try to provide an atmosphere in which
they will become natural by talking to them and stalling when
I have to. Sometimes when they are relaxed I suddenly say,
"Don't move an inch." This drives some people crazy. You
might say that this is unnatural, but the only unnatural thing
is not the pose itself but holding it for so long. There are many
ways. These are mechanics. I might add that I don't only do
portraits. I'm fascinated by pure abstraction, still-life, and
photojournalism—there is no real dividing line between them.
The very word "portrait" seems incorrect to me, too incomplete,
too limiting.

*BC: Could you talk about the space and composition in your
photographs?*

NEWMAN: I was always good at composition when painting.
I loved to play with the flow of line and mass areas. What is
composition? It's the way the picture is pulled together, the
way a picture works. There are no rules and regulations for
perfect composition. If there were we would be able to put all
the information into a computer and would come out with a
masterpiece. We know that's impossible. You have to compose
by the seat of your pants.

  With a few exceptions, the close-up portrait limits what you
can say about a person. The more you show of a person's environment, the more you'll know about the person. Space in
portraiture is interlocked with vision. This is why I watched
with fascination as Mondrian changed the tapes on his painting.
I used to visit him in his apartment studio in 1942 and later.

*BC: You seem to take Mondrianesque care in framing and lining
up your compositions.*

NEWMAN: I learned a great deal just by watching him work.
Once he was working on an unfinished canvas and he turned
to me and asked, "What would you do?" Without hesitation I
said, "I'd move it over about an eighth of an inch that way."
Jeeze, what did I say, I thought as he went over to the canvas.
"Hmmm. I think you're right," he said, and he changed it.
This is not to say that I knew as much as Mondrian, but I
learned a tremendous amount about decision by watching his
work in progress. He gave me two drawings that show the

development towards the final masterpiece, *Broadway Boogie Woogie*. For some reason in photography books, only the finished product is shown. I decided in my book to show a few contact prints because people have asked me questions about the way I made certain photographs. In lectures and class I show failures as well as successes.

BC: What about the symbolism in your work? Is it only related to the sitter or do you try to encompass any larger themes?

NEWMAN: Words like "symbolism" and "realism" and "environmental portraiture" are used as if everything can be premeditated. Things happen to you in a sitting, ideas can be planned but never completely predicted.

BC: What about that skull in the Pollock portrait that is tipped up and staring at him?

NEWMAN: I don't really remember if I moved it or if it was just there. Believe me it wasn't the most important element in the picture and I'm no psychic. I didn't know he was going to die like that. Too many people try to read meaning into accidental elements in photography.

BC: What about the Stravinsky portrait?

NEWMAN: That was one of my more deliberate setups. I had to do some stretching on that because *Harper's Bazaar* asked me to photograph Stravinsky while he was staying in a hotel room. What could I do? I had been looking closely at a piano during a concert a few days before, admiring the harsh, beautiful shapes of the instrument. About that time I did a whole series of abstractions inside the Steinway factory for myself. I began to think about the piano and it struck me that the same kinds of bold curves and angles of the piano were reflected in Stravinsky's own work—strong, harsh and beautiful. An editor at *Harper's Bazaar* let me photograph at her apartment where she had a piano, and the photograph was successful.

I didn't see Stravinsky for several years after that. During that time the damn portrait got reproduced all over the world, to the point where nobody wanted to see my newer work. Finally *Show* magazine asked me to photograph Stravinsky again and I said, "How can I? This damned thing has a life of its own practically." Their reply was, "Well, if you don't do it, we'll send somebody else. . . ." I went. Stravinsky hadn't been well and I remember waiting in the living room after being greeted by Madame Stravinsky. There was a rustle and then I saw Maestro coming in on two canes. He approached me in silence and when he reached me, he put his two canes down very slowly and embraced me, bussing me on both cheeks. With a big grin he said, "Mr. Newman, you have made me famous." I was so touched I almost wept.

But getting back to the question about symbolism: much of it is done unconsciously. Even an attitude of the sitter can be symbolic, such as a gesture of defiance or a gesture of resignation.

BC : Are many people frightened of the camera?

NEWMAN: Frightened or selfconscious, yes. Everyone is, from the president of the United States to the most famous actor. Actors are hard to photograph because they are rarely capable of being themselves.

BC : Aren't people rightfully afraid sometimes, and not just because of the superstition of losing their soul to the little black box?

NEWMAN: You keep talking in terms of loss and ego. People are just selfconscious. You've seen how they fidget with their hands. It's like being put on stage and suddenly you're out there and you're supposed to do something, to be somebody. I have to show my sitters I'm on their side—even if I'm putting the knife in their back the way I did with Krupp. People are relieved if you are sympathetic to their plight of not knowing what to do. Who does know how to pose? I've tried a few self-portraits to finish off the end of a roll of film and I looked like an ass in most of the photographs. I suddenly realized that I needed somebody to direct me. I was as selfconscious as any of my sitters. The real key to being a good photographer is to know people, and I think I do.

BC : Could you attribute this faculty to your childhood experience in the family hotel business?

Newman: Very much so. Plus that business of taking over thirty 49¢ portraits a day where I had to put people at their ease instantly to get results.

BC : Do you normally do limited editions of your work?

Newman: No, but lately I have made some editions. Look, you can print hundreds if you want, but if you ever watch a real photographer work, you see that he agonizes over every print. Not only is it a bore to make hundreds of prints, but it is most uneconomic unless they are pre-sold. I can't spare the time, I want to go on to new work.

BC : Do you do all your printing yourself?

Newman: I have an assistant who helps getting things set up, mostly the mechanical stuff.

BC : How many have you made of the Stravinsky?

Newman: I think it is still under a hundred. I've never kept track. I don't see anything wrong with an artist making money off his art. But he must be reasonable and honest with the public.

BC : How did you develop your cut-outs?

Newman: They were very much a direct response to the early influences on me of Cubist painting. I made the translation of the Cubist approach from one medium to another, but really just to satisfy my own curiosity. I've often thought I should do more work in that area.

BC : Were you trying to emphasize the two-dimensional quality of the photographic image? A kind of retreat from depth of field?

Newman: Not so much as the visual relationships of the components.

JD : What about that tear in the portrait of Claes Oldenburg?

Newman: I took that portrait for *Look* magazine. I was sent to illustrate an article, but I felt the need to go further. I posed Oldenburg in front of his papier-mâché bathtub. Later I saw that it needed something else to make it work, so I tore it. I can't explain why it works, but it does. The incongruity and unexpectedness of the tear helps. I was able to control the tear, but each one was a little different. Some didn't work as well as others. I did about fifteen, destroying most of them and was satisfied with six which I kept. I keep thinking of that quote of Imogen Cunningham: "If you don't like it, that's your problem, not mine." For me, this portrait works. A lot of these things are just inquiries. If you don't have fun, you're not going to get anywhere.

JD : What kind of influence was Stieglitz on you?

NEWMAN: Stieglitz was important to me as a photographer, as a human being, and as a creative person in the art world. He encouraged me photographically and as a human being. The world of art is exciting and there is a lot of exchange. Stieglitz was part of that for me. I was never Stieglitz's protégé and would never pretend to be, but he went out of his way to be nice to me many times after Beaumont Newhall sent me over to him.

When I first arrived in New York, I had spent three years in commercial studios and I'd decided I was going to be a pure artist. I wouldn't touch anything that wasn't as pure as the driven snow. I moved to New York in the fall of '41 broke as hell and a friend of the family called and asked me to do his portrait for about $15. I said fine. "There's only one thing," he said over the phone, "I've got a pimple on my face. You'll be able to retouch it off, won't you?" and he hung up before I could reply. I was good at retouching from my commercial work but I felt I had to be uncompromising in my artistic purity. So as if trying to seek absolution from sin in advance from the Pope, I went over to see Stieglitz. He heard my story and laughed. "Look," he said, "I don't care what you want to do to that negative. If you want to retouch it, spit on it, stamp on it—it doesn't matter. The only thing that matters is the finished picture. If it is honest, it will show it. If it is dishonest, it will show it." He helped set me free of rigid notions.

BC : Did you ever try to apply Stieglitz's ideas to your work?

NEWMAN: To a degree—but you don't have to necessarily be influenced directly or specifically by something in order to be influenced. You may simply be influenced by the excitement generated by some work or idea. You may even dislike something and reject it, but as you accept or reject different ideas that are presented to you, you clarify your own vision. I love Cartier-Bresson's work, but I don't work the way he does. By understanding his work, though, I understand my own better.

Influences come from everywhere but when you are actually shooting, you work primarily by instinct. But what is instinct? It is a lifetime accumulation of influence: experience, knowledge, seeing, and hearing. There is little time for reflection in taking a photograph. All your experiences come to a peak and you work on two levels: conscious and unconscious.

BC: Have you ever found your sitters to be unpleasantly surprised by your portrait of them?

NEWMAN: I think most of them are pleased in a good way by the work I do, especially if they have no preconceived notions about photographs. I've encountered some incredible egos. Just dreadful. Until a few photographers including myself began to do unglamorized, unretouched photographs of executives and politicians, none of them would accept a photograph like that. But once these started appearing in *Life* and became "certified," they learned to accept these images.

BC: Have you ever been unable to make a satisfactory portrait of someone you had personally sought out for a photograph?

NEWMAN: Let's say I've failed on any number of occasions to make a good portrait. If I do fail, I would say that most of the time it is my fault and not my sitter's fault.

JD: You spoke earlier about people learning to appreciate photographs enough to hang them on their walls as art.

NEWMAN: It isn't so much a question of appreciation, but of becoming mentally attuned to the acceptance of photographs as "art." Many people put their photographs on pianos and tables, but they never think of them as creative works, they just think of them as images of something they would like to be reminded of. To them a photograph isn't "arty." An etching is "arty" and a painting is "arty"—certain kinds of painting, that is. Plenty of painters weren't accepted—still aren't—simply because of an attitude at the time.

You can't narrow art to the point where you say this *is* art and this *isn't* art, which means that everything else must be rejected.

Art was meant to be enjoyable and enlightening. I don't feel that everything in photography has to be so serious. There's not enough humor in the world. Have you ever noticed how little humor there is in photography? Very little.

JD: What do you think of some of the trends in photography today?

NEWMAN: Throw me a few names.

BC: Robert Heinecken.

NEWMAN: I bought a Heinecken. He works differently than I do, but I think he is great. I tell my students that I work the way I do because I'm the kind of person that I am. I don't want my students to all end up like little Arnold Newmans. I just try to help them find their own way.

I bought a Bea Nettles and I swapped with Tom Barrow for one of his works. What's wrong with multi-media? Did God come down from above and say that every picture must be a rectangle and be pure without tearing or rearranging of images? No! It's not in the Old or New Testament or the Koran. This kind of attitude comes out of habit and custom. The same is true, as I said before, about hanging photographs on the wall as art.

BC: With the present state of the photography world, will we have to change our ideas about the validity of avant-gardism?

NEWMAN: In any field and at any time, avant-garde is something that happens in relation to time. There's always an avant-garde. The question is: is it really avant-garde or is it someone playing around with gimmicks? It takes a creative mind to see what is avant-garde and what is a gimmick. Gradually a movement begins to settle down on our consciousness and we begin to realize we are being influenced. Very often it is a social influence rather than a creative one as in the case of Andy Warhol who, in my opinion, is somewhat limited. He is not a great artist *per se*, but he led a movement which was comparable to the Dada and Surrealist movements of the Twenties. It was an idea, a social movement rather than what he actually accomplished with his own hands. There are better Pop Artists than he is, but he is a genius as a social force.

A person who is avant-garde is someone who leads others into ideas. Very often someone brilliant doesn't even realize that he's doing it. The real artist is the one that is not so self-conscious about being one step ahead of everyone else. He is simply working on ideas and being himself.

How many new geniuses can we expect each year or each generation? Every year in the art and photography world, there are literally thousands of one-man and one-woman shows. How do we begin to judge? Many are good, but most are simply reworking other people's ideas. How many are the new Stieglitzes, Picassos, Oldenburgs, or Siskinds?

BC: *What do you think of the Photo-Realist painters?*

NEWMAN: They're imitating photography and yet lack the power that photography has of being convincingly real. We know these works were done by painters using a highly pliable medium and we are unable to accept them as absolute realism the way we accept the photographic image. I think they are technically impressive, but that's all. However, Alfred Leslie, Andrew Wyeth, and others don't imitate photography but are nevertheless great realists—so-called "magic realists." Their work has power because it doesn't depend on the utter believability of it. They create pictures that seem real; however, you are not expected to believe in its reality but in its *attitude* of realism.

JD: *Is there anyone right now that you would like to photograph because they have "The Face"?*

NEWMAN: I photograph people, not faces. Of course you go back to the old cliché that "Over fifty, a man makes his own face."

BC : So in thinking photographically you do go beyond the visual?

NEWMAN: I hope to God I do. Otherwise my work would be purely decorative. Let me put it this way: Even the decorative composition must relate in some way or echo, or must at least not be false to the subject matter, whether you are photographing an apple or a scientist or a Nobel Prize-winning author. It's all related.

BC : Is it important to you that your portraits, especially of creative people, be seen together as a series?

NEWMAN: It is not necessary. I didn't intend to make a series of painters, if that's what you mean. As a group of people they offered a great deal of excitement and interest, but I did other kinds of people at the same time.

BC : How do you prefer your work to be seen, in exhibition or in a book?

NEWMAN: They can't be compared and, thank heavens, a choice is not necessary. A book has the advantage that it reaches more people. It's a permanent kind of statement: you can look at it any time you want. The disadvantage is that the reproduction may not be as good and the print is usually reduced in scale, changing our perception of the image. However, both are valid ways of presenting photographs.

Some people say that photographs were made to be reproduced only and that to hang them on walls is pretentious. These people say this because they are only used to seeing them in print. It goes back to what we were saying about being accustomed to a limited view of photography. Certain kinds of pictures were meant to influence opinion and the best way to achieve this is through the media. I remember one critic who said that the photographers at *Life* made photographs only for reproduction, not for exhibit, and that the photographers didn't care what the prints looked like. He had never watched Eugene Smith agonize for two days to get one bloody print! I did.

JD : What knowledge would you want your audience to have when they come to your photographs?

NEWMAN: That's something else. I think it would be stupid of me to expect everyone who comes to look at my photographs to have a knowledge of art or photography. It is my job to please people creatively with some information, some insight, and some emotion. To ask people to have special knowledge would be *chutzpah*. The first person I have to please is myself, then maybe I can please others. If people have knowledge, then that's an additional layer of appreciation, just like going to hear Horowitz if you have studied music.

BC: Your photograph of Stravinsky was originally rejected by Harper's Bazaar. *Did that surprise you at the time?*

NEWMAN: Of course. I just didn't understand why it was rejected. Later I began to realize that Alexey Brodovitch was the kind of art director who liked to have photographs that he could crop and airbrush according to his own ideas of layout. I was not his kind of photographer because arbitrary cropping destroys my work. Years later we asked him to art-direct the first version of my book. To everyone's astonishment, he took my photographs and cropped them. I was saved the embarrassment of saying this would not do when he became ill and could not continue.

BC: What are your feelings about photography's role in the art market?

NEWMAN: I never dreamed that I would be able to derive a large portion of my income from the sale of my prints. I'm rather startled by the reaction in the art market. Will the prices continue to rise? I don't know. Despite the recession, the prints made by some of the famous painters of our time have been artificially pushed up into the thousands of dollars, making it impossible for young collectors who love art to buy them. Some of these people are now turning to photographs although I understand the two markets do not overlap very much. I have deliberately kept my prices down. My gallery, The Light Gallery, convinced me to price my prints so that people can still afford them. I think they're right.

BC: How does a photographer ride the line between his commercial work and his personal work?

NEWMAN: You must be a discerning and analytical critic of

your own work and be able to say, "Okay, here's a damn good job I did commercially, and I'm proud of it as a professional, but it is not art (whatever *that* is). It's simply a good solution to a problem." Commercial photography can be very difficult. Having known people like Weegee, who couldn't separate success from creative achievement, has helped me to understand where I stood. I remember him telling me one night, "Arnold, I'd like to do some really important work. Something really *important* . . . like magazine covers." He never could understand the difference. I'm very proud of some of my professional work. Don't forget that all through history artists in every field have had to work commercially in their art. However, many of my best photographs, like the Stravinsky, were originally made for commercial use. Circumstance enabled me to break loose.

BC: What about the physical permanence of your prints? Does that concern you?

NEWMAN: Yes, because who wants their work to disappear? I remember in 1941 I was talking to Beaumont Newhall in the Museum of Modern Art and Charles Sheeler walked in. Beaumont took the opportunity to show Sheeler a print of his that had already begun to yellow. Sheeler was embarrassed and said, "I made that print ten years ago and didn't know much about washing prints then." He offered to replace it with another print. I vowed to myself then to be careful. Thirty-five years later my prints haven't yellowed or faded. We're still learning a lot about the variables in archival printing, mounting, and storage.

BC: Would you consider printing on platinum paper?

NEWMAN: With all the effort that is required, I would rather put the energy into new projects. I work meticulously so that my silver prints will be permanent. I, like many others, keep trying new materials and methods. Unfortunately, too many manufacturers keep lowering quality or discontinuing products that are not profitable to them.

BC: So photographers are really at the mercy of the commercial suppliers?

NEWMAN: We *are* at the mercy of these companies. If I thought I could make platinum prints right now without breaking my tail, I would. The only one I know who is doing it is Irving Penn. It takes time and money. If someone could produce a high-quality paper right now—even if it cost several times as much as the regular paper—there would be a big enough market of photographers to sell to. I showed by example in a colloquium at the Eastman House recently that the phased-out Kodachrome of 1950 was far superior to the new Ektachrome that replaced it, despite Kodak's counterclaims. It finally happened again recently when K11 Daylight was replaced by K64: it was a disaster. It simply shows that the manufacturers are only interested in money, not quality.

BC : Do you ever travel without your camera?

NEWMAN: I feel naked without it. I can only go for about three days without taking a picture.

JD : Do you find that you see photographically all the time?

NEWMAN: How can one avoid it? I'm always lining things up, measuring angles, even during this interview. I'm observing the way you sit and the way you fit into the composition of the space around you. My friend Chaim Gross, the sculptor, sketches the whole time he's sitting with you. That would be great if I could sketch with a camera like that, and I don't mean with one of those instamatics. It's more complicated than that, though, because every final print demands a follow-through of several hours in the darkroom.

JD : Do you ever wish you had a break from seeing photographically?

NEWMAN: No. I love it too much. I wouldn't be in it if I didn't. If money had been my only aim, there were other ways I could have made more.

BC : To what extent can photography be taught?

NEWMAN: You can't teach any creative medium. All you can hope to do is open a few doors and windows to people. You just try to light a fire under their ass. I try to expose my students to everything from view cameras to 35mm so they get a broad view of what photography is all about.

BC : You've traveled and worked a great deal in Europe. Do you find that the photographer occupies a different status there?

NEWMAN: They're beginning to accept photographers not only as artists but finally as socially acceptable human beings. When I first started working over there, a photographer occupied a position on the social scale just below a plumber. I'm not exaggerating. It was the American photographers who helped alter that. It was different, of course, if you were born in the upper class the way Cecil Beaton was. It is a social world that is entirely different from ours, but it is changing.

BC : Have you ever considered going back to painting?

NEWMAN: Every time I smell oil paint, I'm like a race horse— I want to get started again. The only reason that I don't is that I have a horror of being second-rate. It would take me years to get back to a point where I wouldn't be an embarrassment to myself.

BC : Do you think it would be figurative or abstract?

NEWMAN: Who knows? Intellectually I know that unless I could add something to it, figurative painting wouldn't quite do it for me. I'd be expected to be good and I couldn't treat it as a hobby. You know, a doctor who is a friend of mine suggested that to relieve tension I should take up carpentry. "But don't use anything smaller than a 2 by 4, otherwise you'll get too involved," he told me. That's the way I am.

BC : Where do you go from here photographically?

NEWMAN: If I knew, I'd be there already. At the moment I'm still groping.

Lord Snowdon

Lord Snowdon (Antony Armstrong-Jones) was born in England in 1930. Educated at Eton and Cambridge, he began photographing while at school, and at the age of twenty went to serve as assistant to the society photographer Baron.

From 1959 his work has appeared in many magazines, most notably *Vogue*, *Harper's Bazaar*, and *The Sunday Times Magazine*. An energetic and innovative man, Snowdon is credited with being the first of a new breed of fashion photographers, bringing the candid sensibility of the photojournalist to the pages of fashion magazines.

In the fifties and sixties, he concentrated on travel and portrait work, publishing books on Malta and London, and collaborating with John Russell and Bryan Robertson for the book *Private View*, a study of the English art world. Since the sixties he has turned more frequently to social problems in his choice of subjects, his documentary work including photo essays on old age, the mentally ill, loneliness, and the physically handicapped.

Snowdon's achievements in other fields are also noteworthy. He has designed a wheelchair for the disabled, and an aviary for the London Zoo where for the first time the birds are able to fly around and be seen in what is almost a natural habitat. His documentary films on old age, people's dependency on

animals, and the problems of small people, have earned praise on both sides of the Atlantic.

In 1972, he was commissioned by Olivetti to photograph Venice, resulting in the book *A View of Venice*. His exhibition *Assignments* (also a book), has been seen in England, Australia and the United States.

In April, 1976, at Snowdon's photography exhibition in Australia, a man pulled out a knife and slashed a picture of Elizabeth Taylor across the face. In a year that had seen the destruction of a Rembrandt and a Picasso, it seemed one more way—peculiar but not incongruous—for photography to join the ranks of the other visual arts. When I mentioned the incident to Lord Snowdon (before I turned the tape on) in the context of seeing photography on a level with the masterpieces that had been vandalized, he disregarded the notion and politely changed the subject. There was no room in his view of photography for a question as pretentious as that.

I interviewed Lord Snowdon on an April day in London in a basement flat off Belgrave Square. Dressed in a dark green corduroy suit and turtleneck, he looked slighter than I had expected; and although his features are boyish-looking individually, on that day he looked careworn—a man besieged by deadlines and gossip.

Inside the sparsely furnished flat, the only pictures I could see were one of a white horse's head and two large black-and-white photographs of his children. As I set up my tape recorder on his desk, we talked about recording equipment, and he looked around the study to show me a microphone that Sony had adapted to his specifications. One alteration he had made was simply to have it painted from silver to black. "It's less distracting that way," he explained.

Before we began, he showed me proofs of some pictures for a Sunday Times Magazine *article on children in prison. In the photographs where some of the children's features would have been too clearly recognizable, the faces had been crudely shaded down, with an eye to efficiency rather than delicacy.*

When I turned the tape on for the interview, he first had me check it to make sure it was working. He was completely at ease with the recorder, and he seemed totally unaware of it until either the phone rang or he had something to say that was off the record or not relevant. "You can turn the tape off for a bit," he would say without missing a beat, and in the same tone, he would tell me when to turn it on again. We talked this way for over three hours.

JD: *Were you in Australia when your photograph of Elizabeth Taylor was slashed?*

SNOWDON: Yes.

JD: *What did you make of that?*

SNOWDON: Well, the moral of that story is: always answer letters. The man who did it was in love with her from afar and he had written her a letter which she hadn't answered, so that was what prompted it. He came in to the exhibition and got out some kind of knife and just slashed it. He was then spotted by security men and chased through the exhibition down into the street. When they caught up with him, he lashed out and stabbed one of the security men in the neck. I wasn't there at the time, so I rushed out to the hospital and luckily, the security man was all right. If it had been another quarter of an inch deeper, he might have been dead.

I then went back to the exhibition, and there was this young photographer there and he said, "For heaven's sake, leave the photograph slashed, it's made it much more interesting." So I left it there.

JD : Isn't the way in which the exhibition is set up—the order in which the photographs are seen—very important to you?

SNOWDON: Yes. I set it up so that you wander round in a certain shape, usually keeping to sixty degrees or one hundred and twenty. Then when you walk through it, if you look to the right, you see the escapist things of life, and if you look to the left, you see the realities of life (the social-problem pictures).

It's not a photographer's exhibition. You come out of it, I think, with a slightly depressing feeling about life, but you don't come out knowing any more about stops and lighting and film and all the rest of it.

JD : You have said, "The point of photography is to make ordinary people react."

SNOWDON: Yes. That's what I said in 1958, which is a hell of a long time ago. To me, photography is to move people, to make people think, but never, never at the expense of the person you are photographing. To laugh with, yes—but never to laugh at.

The thing about the pictures like the ones of mental health, or old age, or the latest ones of children in prison, is that the photographer is secondary to the writer. He's there to illustrate, like a cartoonist: to emphasize certain things perhaps, but above all to make people read the piece. For me, a photographic book fails if it doesn't have a lot of text. It becomes impractical.

If one can just make ordinary people aware of certain things . . . as I was saying just now, there are in Britain 4,000 kids in prison—half of them haven't been proved guilty at all. They are made to wear uniforms, they are looked after by uniformed officers, and of course that will start them off on a road to crime if you're not very careful.

JD : The relationship between you and the writer must then be of great importance.

SNOWDON: Yes, it becomes a very, very close thing and I've been lucky enough to always work with writers that I've got on with. It's a relationship of knowing when to shut up and listen to him doing an interview, having discussions all the time; me doing my homework beforehand and seeing the various ways one could do this and that. Some photographers think that writers shouldn't interfere and suggest things—I think that two brains are better than one.

JD : It seems to me that with your social-problem photographs, you keep away from the dramatic pictures and approach the subject in a more gentle way. Do you find this a more effective approach?

SNOWDON: Well, I don't think I do it consciously. I'm not out to shock, though—it's too easy to shock. There's one photographer—who will remain nameless—whose work I loathe, I actually detest, because it is a voyeur's: out to make fun of and to laugh at, and to shock in a horrid kind of way. Again, you're not always aware of why you take pictures in a certain way, but I hope that my pictures aren't recognizable and that I don't have a style. If I do have a style, then that's my failing.

What I want is for people to know more about the subject. Of course, all human beings have certain things that they believe in—and obviously over the years you do, I suppose, sub-consciously take things in a certain way. But I do think if you take a horrifying subject that needs a lot of thought, and you take it in a fairly soft way, you can softly get people to look at it. The mental-health piece, for example, I called "Caring for the Mentally Sick," so there was nearly always a nurse in the picture. Like the one with the nurse kneeling down with the little girl—it was that relationship of caring one used to draw attention to the problem of mental health.

JD : Have you ever photographed a war?

SNOWDON: No, I haven't, but I admire Don McCullin's work enormously. I think he would have the same sort of feeling about this too; but his pictures have to be shocking, have to be horrifying. I think that war pictures have got to come back and be published to help prevent other atrocities of that kind happening. That's their object, to my way of thinking—not to be horror pictures to sell newspapers or magazines. They have to be hard, very hard, but I would hope that Don would say that he does it because he just wants to illustrate that ghastly side of life for people not to sweep under the mat.

142

JD : To get to the beginning of your photographic career for a while, had you always wanted to be a photographer?

SNOWDON: No, not at all. I was more of an engineer/plumber type child, liking photography as a machine, liking developing and printing. Then at school I started a photographic society, and then went to Cambridge. I was going to go to M.I.T., but I changed and went to Cambridge to read Natural Sciences, which I did for all of ten days and loathed it. After that I changed to Architecture. I had to come down from Cambridge because I failed my exams and I hadn't finished my portfolio. I meant to go back again but then just drifted into taking photographs. I thought at one time of going into my grandfather's business in the City, but I'd have been useless as a stockbroker.

JD : When you were twenty, you went to work for Baron.

SNOWDON: Yes. I was there for about six months and it was useful in lots of ways. He was doing mostly ladies against tapestries, mounted and hand tinted and everything else, portrait gallery stuff which I really don't like at all, but it gave me the insight of how a studio worked. He had a formula for lighting: there were two lights on the head from behind, another one to light the hands, one to light the face with a little shadow, and another little inky-dinky to fill in. All this had absolutely nothing to do with what I think the use of the camera is about because it was really a form of cheap painting; but I learned a lot there, and it was well worth the two pounds I was paid a week!

JD : Was it after that when you did photographs for the theater?

SNOWDON: Yes. What happened in those days was that there were photographs outside the theaters, little 8x10 glossies. You set up one scene and everyone had to be in it in the right kind of way, and then outside the theater, you had this tiny little displayer photograph. Anyway, through the patronage of George Devine at the Royal Court, and the patronage of Toby Roland and various other people, I was allowed to do different things. Sometimes I would photograph during the rehearsals, or during the performances in the provinces. Other times I would take things outside the theater altogether but in the mood of the play, and then I would dress the theater with huge blow-ups of photographs that were very grainy but gave, for the first time, movement. They weren't sharp, the actresses weren't retouched, but it was the first time there was a kind of reality in these pictures. Certain actresses really hated it, but I think I did what my job as I saw it was—to get people off the bus to go and buy a ticket and see the play . . . which is really the same as what one's trying to do in a magazine now.

JD : What about your films? The first was Don't Count the Candles.

SNOWDON: Yes. That was about the aspects and problems of old age. The second one was called *Love of a Kind*, it was about loneliness and dependency on animals, and the next one was *Born to be Small*, which again clarifies what we were talking about earlier in that it concerns that hairline of what is acceptable and what is not. I think it worked because all the people who were in it who were small wrote to me afterwards and thanked me for making for more understanding, saying that since the films, people have treated them as equals.

During the making of that, I had to take certain scenes out of sequence which, if edited in the wrong way, would have been far too shocking. There was one sequence right at the end where somebody who was very small—she was twenty-nine inches high—went to a dance with other small people, and I shot that first. Then we did an interview with her, and in the interview she said how much she'd enjoyed the dance. Well there we changed the order so one established her character first in the interview and then did the dancing sequence so that you were in no way laughing at or exposing her to anything except for understanding.

JD : Do you ever see film becoming more important to you than still photography?

SNOWDON: No. I'll always go back to stills. On the other hand, I would like to do more documentaries, more films, but always with the smallest kind of crew. I would never do (not that I've been asked to) a big film in a studio. To make a great epic would appall me. You see, film does not come naturally to me. I suppose it's because having been brought up for so long to think about moments, you don't think of the flow of things.

The other thing I hate with film is that you can't crop. You're stuck with the thing you've actually shot. On a lot of the photographs I take, I may take out a small corner that I like and use that bit only; or if I find something in a photograph that I don't like—a lamp post, or whatever—then certainly I will retouch it out. I try to make all my photographs as simple as possible, and I like to get the viewer's eye to go straight to the most important bit in the photograph and not be distracted by irrelevant things. I hate any piece of light that is unimportant on the edge of a photograph, and I will darken or print it down.

JD: Your book, Assignments, *seems to me to be extremely carefully laid-out both graphically and editorially. Was that an important part of the book?*

SNOWDON: Yes. Layout is extremely important to me. I can't bear it when people look at a book of mine in front of me, but if they do, and they look at it backwards, that irritates me dreadfully. The Venice book, for example, was designed to be just a day in Venice, starting early morning, and going through to the night. It should be seen almost like a film, your eye taking you from one image to another with the photographs relating to each other in some way. Again, with the Venice book, I would cheat—and it is cheating—by altering colors. Sometimes by chance something goes wrong and looks better because of a mistake. In the Venice book, I would match up the colors in one spread and use the same reds. Now that meant working very closely with the printers in Switzerland and it took about a year to complete.

I don't like doing layouts, however, and indeed couldn't do layouts by myself. If you've taken the photographs, you have got too many things in the back of your mind about the condition of a sitting or an assignment that may blur what's important or what you're trying to get at. So you want a close relationship with somebody whom you can have strong arguments with. The worst thing would be to have a sycophantic art director. You want someone with whom you can argue, explain why you did it, and then get out of their hair, and they will then say, "No, I don't agree with that, I've done it like this."

JD: Assignments *opens with a romantic color picture of two whales and closes with a stark black-and-white of two petrified bodies. How important is that symbolism meant to be?*

SNOWDON: Very few people notice things like that, and I certainly don't want to thrust it down their throat. People can take those photographs and read a kind of symbolism into them, or they can not notice it.

JD : Would you employ that symbolism today?

SNOWDON: I don't think you ever do the same thing twice—or hopefully not—because you know when you've done something, you've always done it wrong. It's like doing a building—somebody asked me if I were to do the birdcage at the zoo again, would I do it the same way? The answer is: of course not, because I don't like it. It's the same with photographs—the older they are, the more you hate them; and it is that strange thing about taking photographs that you always live in hope that you're going to get something that you're pleased with, and somewhere along the line, it always goes wrong. From the moment you start taking pictures, and when you start an assignment, you live this butterfly existence. You meet somebody you think you know enough about and you do the best you can within that brief space of time you've been given. Then you need to see the pictures very quickly, you want them processed fast, and there's the dread of opening the envelope because you know you haven't got it. Then you think, well, maybe when it's enlarged and I cut out this and retouch that, it will be better, but it never is. I suppose that if you did do a picture that you were pleased with, then you would give up.

With the whale picture, again, I think it's quite a nice baroque shape, which is luck. It's all luck, the whole thing. There, maddeningly, the tail's cut off, which I don't like, but if you're underwater with a couple of seventeen-foot whales, you can't tell them to pose.

JD : Is there one place which seems to you to be the proper domain for photographs—an exhibition, or in a book, framed in someone's house?

SNOWDON: Never framed, never treated with reverence. I'm terribly against this pretentious thing of having a limited

146

number of prints done and destroying the negative. I think this is unbelievably conceited arrogance. And when people in the fine arts, when painters are doing more and more posters, more and larger runs so more members of the public can enjoy the fine arts, why should photographers be conceited enough to try and do short runs to make money? I'm absolutely against that. I'm against photographs being signed and sold as a work of art. They aren't. They should be looked at in a magazine and then used to wrap up the fish and chucked away. I suppose you can put a bit of glass over a picture if you want to keep the dust off, but you know, it's only worth the paper it's printed on.

I think it's important to keep all negatives because they'll be quite interesting in three or four hundred years time—if they haven't all faded—as a record of what was going on, but I'm amazed by all these photographs that fetch a lot of money. I don't understand that. If you've got the negative, do another print and shove it in a magazine.

JD: When you did the Venice book, did you stop and think of your work in an art-historical context? I mean there's an enormous tradition.

SNOWDON: It scared one stiff, yes. I know Venice quite well—I used to go there with my uncle a lot in the fifties, and loved it—but I'm terrified of it photographically because every time you look around, you get a Canaletto.

Olivetti first asked me to do it in black-and-white, and I went out on one trip and I thought, "in no way"; so I changed to color, which put up their expenses rather a lot. To answer your question, though, I tried to avoid, except at the very end, all the things that most commonly appear in picture books of Venice. [The end piece is a photograph of a stand with post-cards of all the famous Venetian scenes.]

JD: When people look at photographs, to what extent do you think that they are bound in by the aesthetics of painting? If people look at a photograph as a painting, does this bother you?

SNOWDON: Yes, it does dreadfully. If somebody very kindly says, "Oh, lovely photograph, it's just like a painting," then I take that as absolutely my failing because then it should be a painting. This is said quite often about one picture of mine of a picnic in Peru, and I admit it is like a rather bad late nineteenth-century painting that you might find, with clouds in the sky and all the rest of it. Actually, somebody wrote to me when I was in Australia and said that they'd seen my exhibit and they liked my paintings very much. That was not good.

JD : Do you think that there is anything you can do about that?

SNOWDON: No. The viewer is right and I'm wrong. I think the photograph has got to speak absolutely for itself: the photographer shouldn't have to say anything about it, and that's why captions can sometimes ruin a photograph. People say that most of my pictures are sad. I don't think that's true. I hope that sometimes I do pictures to make people laugh, but again, funny because of the situation, not laughing at.

JD : In the book In Vogue, *you are called the first of the send-up photographers, and your work is characterized as "outrageous moments caught by the camera when no one should have been looking." What was your attitude to doing fashion?*

SNOWDON: Basically, I didn't like doing fashion pictures. I was always being forced to by *Vogue,* so I used to have fun with it. I didn't want to do that kind of posed studio thing and so did send it all up, and had great fun doing it.

It's done a lot today. I didn't know that they said I was the first, but I remember I was asked to photograph some luggage once by *Vogue,* so I threw it all out a window into a beautiful open car below. Again, it was the same as doing things for the theater—it was making people stop to look at the page, hopefully in a new kind of way.

I did some dancing photographs where people were on ropes upside down, and their shoes were nailed to the floor, and then I'd retouch the ropes out so they were defying gravity. I just had fun, really, doing it in a very flippant way. I couldn't take the fashion thing very seriously, however, even though I love clothes. I love clothes by people like Zandra Rhodes and Bill Gibb but I don't want to photograph them very much. . . . I designed a collection of ski clothes once, though. I don't think anyone bought them, but again, it was great fun to do, and in those days, you see, people were wearing sort of golfing clothes to go skiing in. Mine had all these big belts and buckles, but they were at the wrong time. It's not clever to be ahead of your time. It's worse than being behind the time, really, because nobody wants them. You want to be just a little bit ahead. Like in motorcar design, if you designed a car which was twenty years ahead, it wouldn't be clever, it would just be wrong timing. You want to advance little by little, otherwise the public won't accept it.

JD : What satisfaction do you get from portraiture?

SNOWDON: Absolutely none from photographing somebody for themselves.

JD : What is the challenge then?

SNOWDON: Trying to get something that is typical. It doesn't give me pleasure to just photograph a face. To photograph somebody because they want to be photographed and stick it in a silver frame on the piano, that I would hate to do except when I need the money. The challenge is to photograph somebody in the mood that tells the viewer something more about that person that is typical.

I saw the other day in a photographic magazine a portrait of somebody and the caption said, "This is a portrait of so and so as he's never been seen before." Well now, that is the complete opposite of my thinking. If you photograph somebody as they've never been seen before, which means untypical, then I don't understand that. I want to photograph somebody as typically as I can.

JD : Taking your photograph of Calder, if you didn't know what Calder looked like, and you looked at the picture for long enough, you might be able to guess who it was. Does that make it a successful picture for you?

SNOWDON: Again, that was luck. It was luck in that I don't think he meant his cooking things to look like mobiles—it just happened. I'd done a lot of other pictures of him in his studio but they were boring. This was one after we'd finished and had lunch, and we'd had some wine, and he was dancing and she was playing the accordion, and it was suddenly him. If it works, yes, that's lovely. Things like that happen.

There were some pictures I did of Nabokov when he was

staying in a hotel in Switzerland. The hotel was nothing, the room was awful—there was no way that it seemed to make any sense about him. We went onto the roof of the hotel because I wanted just a plain white, no scene background to start off with, and by chance, in the sign with the name of the hotel one letter had fallen off, so it apparently meant something else in Russian, which is exactly the sort of word tricks that he does. Nabokov noticed it, and he said, "Heavens, behind me, look. That means so and so in Russian backwards." It's odd. I believe in those strange days when you are lucky; when things happen . . . but quite often they don't.

JD : Are you often surprised by what you see after you've taken the picture, when you're looking at the contacts?

SNOWDON: Oh yes, absolutely. You notice certain things in the contacts that you hadn't actually noticed with your eye. I also think with proofs and contacts you can read the way an assignment went. In an assignment that went well, you'll see you suddenly have an idea and then work on that idea again and again and again, for hours around about it and the pictures will all be almost exactly the same. If an assignment is going badly, then you're darting around all over the place, and you know something's gone wrong because all the contacts are different. If it's going well, there's maybe just one picture out of it.

JD : Do you have any favorite sitters? I noticed that you have series of both Alec Guiness and Laurence Olivier.

SNOWDON: Again, that was by chance because over twenty years, you see, I photographed quite a lot of people several times. Alec Guiness I remember photographing very early on when I had a studio in Pimlico. I was absolutely terrified. Here was this great star coming to me to be photographed as himself. Well, he's one of those people whom you've seen in so many different parts, you don't know exactly who he is. He's enormously shy, and a shy person always makes you shyer; so there was this agonizing, terrifying experience of photographing him not as a part, but as a faceless, kind person. That was a difficult one, but mostly it's a matter of people with whom you can immediately get on the same wavelength, and then it

150

can be marvelous. There are other people who can be just a bit sticky because you're not on the same wavelength.

JD : When you're taking photographs, are you aware of the camera at the moment you press the shutter release?

SNOWDON: No, absolutely not. The camera is the one thing I don't like. First of all it makes a noise. Secondly, it's visible, and so it destroys your getting that moment. Doing documentary type things, if a photograph is underexposed or overexposed, or out of focus, that, to me, is secondary to the moment. I take the picture when I first see it. Then maybe I'll have a little bit more time to focus and set it right. But it's the first one that is the real moment even though it may be technically bad.

I do work with two cameras—each with a different lens— but it's a disadvantage to have two cameras because people look at you. Most people don't walk around with two cameras round their neck, so you become a visible watcher.

In the last twenty years, people have become far more aware of being photographed. This happens especially in places like Africa. In America I don't think they notice so much.

I was asked by *McCalls* to photograph the Amish people. Now that was a difficult assignment to do because it is against their religion to have electric light, or radio, or a telephone and all that; and they're a beautiful race of people, but they don't want to be photographed—or shouldn't be.

Anyway, first of all I found out there was a book about them, so they had been photographed, and I went down to Pennsylvania and luckily met several of them who didn't mind being photographed. I did those as totally posed pictures to show all the other Amish if they saw it that they had agreed to pose. With the other pictures that I took of the Amish people, I thought it was all right if they became anonymous within the environment. Hopefully that worked, because a lot of them wrote to me and thanked me for doing it in that way. And I hope it might have made for a little more understanding from amateurs who go there and just put cameras in people's faces and photograph them.

JD : How then do you deal with the intruding aspect of the camera if you're given a social problem assignment where you feel that it is necessary for you to take a certain picture because it might be able to do some good?

SNOWDON: I'm very aware of the problem, obviously, and it's really a matter of taste and judgment, and having the trust of the person you're photographing. I have photographs that I've had to take, but wouldn't publish because I thought they were an intrusion. With the "Children in Prison" piece, there are some pictures where I can see their faces perhaps a little bit too much, which I didn't realize at the time, and so now those will be destroyed.

Privacy is vitally important, I think, and this sort of long-lens sneaky stuff I won't go along with at all. I think it's perfectly all right to use a very long lens provided you give the person you're photographing a walkie-talkie and you've contacted them. I do that sometimes with pictures to get a certain visual perspective. A long lens is for photographing animals or sport, but not people who are unaware. Somebody should have the right not to be photographed if they don't want to be.

I think that it's quite wrong to photograph, for example, Garbo, if she doesn't want to be photographed. Now I would have loved to photograph her, but she obviously didn't want to be photographed so I didn't follow it up. Then somebody will photograph her walking down the street because she has to walk down the street, and I mind that sort of intrusion. I think this is horrible. This sort of *papparazzi* thing is harmful to journalism.

JD : What do you think of some of the directions that photography is taking today? The conceptual work that one sees in the galleries?

SNOWDON: I hate them, especially when they're trying to be arty. I don't like photographs in galleries much; and I don't like photographic galleries. I saw the photographic exhibition that was done last year at the Royal College of Art and I thought they were quite dreadful. They were pretentious things and you felt the students wanted to do painting. They were sticking bits of hair on photographs and doing all sorts of things—tearing them up, you know—it was so phony. I thought it was ridiculous, but if they want to do it, that's their business. I just don't happen to want to.

I think it's perfectly all right and very good when you're at the age of eighteen to twenty-four to do all those silly things, to get it out of your system. What happens when you get to, say forty-six like I am now, is that you can't be doing those things—it's got to be simpler and simpler and simpler. This doesn't mean it gets better, but it's got to try and get to a certain truth.

But photography has had such an effect on painting—it actually wrecked the livelihoods of the painters who were recordists, and to reverse it now, in the way that they're trying to be influenced by painting is, I think, silly.

JD : Which gets us back to what you said in the beginning about the role of the photographer being just to make ordinary people react.

SNOWDON: Yes, as a straight journalist, really. I think I said, "To laugh, sometimes to cry, never to wince. . . ." I can't remember the rest.

JD : Apart from being a photographer, you are an inventor, designer . . .

SNOWDON: Failed architect, I think.

JD : If you were not able to photograph any more, would these other things be fulfilling to you?

SNOWDON: Well, I think one would readjust oneself, but I hope that won't happen yet. If I couldn't take photographs, I don't know what I would do.

JD : When everything has been considered, is it the social-problem photography that is the most important to you?

SNOWDON: Yes, but it's only become more important with age. I mean it wasn't there nearly so much when I was twenty. And between twenty and thirty, I wasn't doing it really. It's only happened over the last decade. I think that is the way life goes—it just changes. I still want to go back to doing light things occasionally. One mustn't always do the heavy scene because I think it becomes too much. You know?

Brett Weston

Brett Weston was born in Los Angeles in 1911, the second son of the great photographer Edward Weston. He began photography under his father's tutelage while the two were living together in Mexico. Within a few years he was exhibiting his own work and in 1930 had his first one-man show at Jake Zeitlin's gallery in Los Angeles.

In order to support his personal work, Brett Weston made his living for a time as a professional portrait photographer. He also worked briefly in Hollywood as a cameraman, and was a photographer for the Farm Security Agency.

When Edward Weston was stricken with Parkinson's disease in the late 1940's, Brett often gave time to projects involving his father's work. In 1952 he participated in the printing of eight portfolios from the thousand negatives that Edward Weston considered his best work.

Brett Weston has had numerous exhibitions of his photographs, including one-man shows at the San Francisco Museum and the Museum of Modern Art. He has published two books, *Brett Weston: Photographs* and *A Voyage of the Eye*.

When twenty-year-old Brett Weston was trying to earn a living as a portrait photographer in Santa Barbara during the Depression, he sometimes wore a black beret and cape, swung a black cane, and

whizzed along the coast roads in a Packard sports car. Despite
these flamboyant trappings of bohemia and apparent success,
Weston was subsisting on $50 a month—dinner often consisted of
the number of canapés he could stuff in his pocket at cocktail parties
in Montecito.

Forty years later, a more spartan Weston greeted me at the
door of his modern house overlooking the Carmel Valley. He was
of medium height and stockily built, dressed simply in khakis and
a short sleeved work shirt. His handsome face was red from the
sun and he wore dark glasses. In his left hand he held a beer and I
noticed that all the fingernails were black, stained by developer.
He had been up since 4 a.m. in the darkroom.

The house was airy and sparingly furnished with a couple of
sling chairs, two pre-Columbian stone figures and six or seven of
the organic shaped sculptures that Weston has carved over the
years. Except for two small paintings in the bedroom, the rest of
the wallspace of the house was devoted entirely to a score of recent
Weston photographs that were hung like a gallery exhibit. The
absence of human clutter gave the house the feel of a weekend
retreat, rather than of a permanent residence.

Weston was difficult to interview. His unwillingness to answer
some of the questions dealing with symbolism or philosophy seemed
justified somehow in his reply: "I'm just a photographer. I'm not

too verbal. This is my language." He pointed to the photographs on the walls.

He seemed quite comfortable, however, talking about non-photographic subjects. His voice was brusque but had an educated, almost professorial tone to it. While his young apprentice Dianne Nelson fixed cold drinks, he talked animatedly about bullfights he had seen in his youth in Mexico with his father, Edward Weston. "The spectacle fascinated and impressed me profoundly. I never tried to photograph it though. What correlation there is between bullfighting and photography I couldn't say, but we're influenced by everything."

Weston seemed relieved when the interview was over and showed me the darkroom off the living room. There was a sign on the door that said "Private." Like the rest of the house, the darkroom was neat and uncluttered.

Before I left, Weston took me out to the garage and showed me the Camera Car—one of several vans he has used over the years to transport his photography equipment. "Ansel Adams is touring Scotland right now in a Rolls Royce with a chauffeur. When I go over next month, I'll be in a VW bus." A few minutes later, Weston excused himself and went back to the darkroom to test out some new equipment.

BC : Do you remember your first photograph?

WESTON: Vividly. I was electrified by my first image. I used my father's old Graflex, a 3¼x4¼ on a tripod in Mexico when I was twelve years old. He gave me very brief instructions and an idea of the exposure because we had no light meters in those days. We had to judge the light from the back of the camera. I was simply staggered by that image on ground glass.

BC : Do you still get that feeling today?

WESTON: It's stronger now than ever before. Of course, it's more assured now.

BC : What was that first picture?

WESTON: It was a magnolia bud, a closeup. I'd seen my father's work briefly, having been virtually weaned on hypo,* but I

---

*Hypo is a common name for fixer, which is the chemical compound used to preserve the image on a developed negative.

seemed to have a natural rapport with the photographic image. Even before that I used to draw on my own—instinctively. I've always had the feeling that artists are born and not created in art schools. Art schools are fine for technique but the rest is just bunk and bullshit.

BC : Even though the camera is a mechanical device?

WESTON: The camera for an artist is just another tool. It is no more mechanical than a violin if you analyze it. Beyond the rudiments, it is up to the artist to create art, not the camera.

BC : You reached a degree of excellence very early in your life. Did you ever wonder after the first successes how you did it?

WESTON: I never intellectualized it or gave it too much thought. It was a very instinctive, built-in thing. It was a way of seeing life. I just went ahead and photographed. But don't get me wrong: my work is not simple. It is highly complex, especially now.

BC : You said once that "Intellectualization is my sworn enemy."

WESTON: Well not exactly . . . I appreciate a good intellect, God knows, but I'm not verbal about it. It comes out in my work, in my photography. It takes too much energy to write about it.

BC : Have you ever considered any other form of expression beside photography?

WESTON: Sculpture. I've done that for many years as a kind of therapy. After long hours in the darkroom with the acid fumes and hypo, you get claustrophobia. So I get out my power tools, my chisels, and files and hack on wood. I've been doing it for forty years.

BC : It sounds as if your sculpture comes out of a need to have a counterbalance to the delicacy of photographic expression.

WESTON: It's a nice change of pace. One influenced the other and often I would plagiarize myself, in a sense. Certain forms

157

in my photography would influence the sculptural forms, which you can see if you look at my sculpture.

BC : Could you talk about your father?

WESTON: Number one, he was a magnificent parent: a wonderful father and a great friend. Even as a boy of fifteen I knew he was a great artist. I just felt this. His work enthralled me. I was influenced by his work for the first couple of years, but I think we had a very different kind of vision ultimately. He influenced me strongly with regard to technique. We are a progression, all a part of the human stream, and there is no escaping influence. What is important is what we add to it from ourselves. We lived together and traveled together for maybe eight to ten years, then I spread my wings and flew off to Los Angeles and to Santa Barbara when I was eighteen. For a time though we worked closely together in San Francisco and Los Angeles in a joint studio. I developed his film and printed his commercial portraits.

BC : Did you ever reach a point in your association where you felt selfconscious or cramped as an artist developing your father's work?

WESTON: Well, I didn't develop his personal work, just the commercial portraits. We had to do this for bread and butter. It was purely a business venture, a matter of survival.

BC : You have three brothers—Chandler, Cole, and Neil. I understand Cole has also worked in photography.

WESTON: Chan was involved originally. He is my older brother by two years. He went to Mexico with my father in 1923 and started out brilliantly. Dad thought he would be the artist in the family—the photographer—but he got sidetracked into politics and drew away from it in part because of the emotional problems involved with the separation of my mother and father.

Cole has been very active, especially in printing my father's work for the last twenty years or so. He's not totally dedicated to photography. He's done many things from politics to theater, but he's apparently starting to photograph more and more.

BC: It is interesting that, as the second son, you should end up as the photographer. Were you closer to him than the other boys?

WESTON: He loved all his sons equally for different reasons. We were perhaps closer aesthetically and visually, and we seemed to respond to the same sort of people. Our way of life was quite similar, fairly ascetic and spartan.

BC: I understand it was you who suggested that your father change from palladium and platinum prints to the glossy bromide paper.

WESTON: I didn't really suggest it. The platinum is a matte surface and doesn't reveal everything that's in the negative the way the glossy paper does. We had it lying around the studio for proof sheets and I just began to use it. I didn't argue with him about it—you didn't argue with Edward Weston—I just said, "Dad, I like it." Pretty soon he started using it, too.

BC: He wrote in his Daybook *that you influenced him a great deal.*

WESTON: Yes, but he was such a big man that he would say I influenced him. He was also a very humble man. He realized that I had my own vision and my own thoughts and he left me alone. He never tried to interfere. He would just tell me whether he liked my work or not. Of course that affected me, naturally, but so did his enthusiasm, which directed me.

BC: Your father also wrote in his Daybook *that "Brett and I see things the same way; we have the same kind of vision."*

WESTON: I think what he meant was that we responded to the same kind of subject matter; but our interpretation was very different.

BC: In what way does your vision differ?

WESTON: Mine is more complicated now, perhaps more abstract.

BC: Does your daughter Erica do any work in photography with such a heritage behind her?

159

WESTON: No. Perhaps she was too steeped in it. I would have encouraged her if she had wanted to do it. I'm the only one in the family totally committed to photography.

BC: Did your early involvement with photography cut you off from what might be considered a "normal" childhood?

WESTON: I would think so. I was a misfit even in grammar school—the original dropout at twelve years old, rebelling against the regimentation. Dad just took me to Mexico where I had some informal tutoring. I'm still weak in arithmetic and spelling. In fact, I spell better in Spanish. But I read a great deal and was introduced to marvelous people and this became my education, along with photography. We were there during that Renaissance in Mexico when the painters Diego Rivera and Clemente Orozco held forth—these people and others contributed to my growth and background.

BC: Orozco and Rivera were quite political at the time. Did this affect you at all?

WESTON: Dad was antagonized by the Communist scene during that period. Tina Modotti, his mistress . . . the lovely Tina . . . got involved in 1926 with the Party and Dad just couldn't stomach this. He was very humanistic—he loved people—but he could not stand the idea of the regimentation involved. You get this regimentation whether it's Red China or Hitler or Stalin—it's the same old crap with just a different handle on it.

BC: Did this political polarity contribute to the break-up between Tina and your father?

WESTON: Yes. Well, they outgrew each other. They were together for three years and Dad, you know, was always pursuing someone else. We were close friends and I thought she was a fine person in many ways.

BC: There's a book out now on her life and work. She learned photography from your father.

WESTON: A lot of people think she was a great photographer, but she wasn't. She had only two years' experience and was really just a beginner with a great potential which was never exploited. She had a good eye, but it was political and turned more and more to the Left. She finally got sidetracked by politics.

BC : You judge the greatness of a photographer not on the brilliance of, say, a handful of prints but on a body of work from a lifetime? Not from a single masterpiece, as has sometimes been the case of certain writers or painters?

WESTON: You can't be considered great on the power of a single photograph.

BC : During the Depression you were a supervisor for twenty photographers under the Federal Arts Project. What happened to those people? Did they ever make it as photographers?

WESTON: Not one that I can recall.

BC : What did you do with them on the Project?

WESTON: So-called "creative photography." I'd just say, "Hey, fellows, let's go out and photograph." We were on the dole. I was the so-called "supervisor" and had a secretary whom I used to flirt with. One guy, Leroy Robbins, had a good eye but he got sidetracked into the motion picture industry.

BC : Weren't you a cameraman for Twentieth-Century-Fox yourself?

WESTON: Briefly. I was a remote assistant cameraman. I was draft-dodging. Then I got so bored with that crap that I called my draft board from the sound stage and told them I'd rather be in the Army. I was making a lot of money but there was the worst stuff going on in Hollywood.

BC : Did the medium of film appeal to you?

WESTON: I love film but I'm a still photographer. As a matter of fact though, there are three people doing films on me right now. But it's a completely different art form. I couldn't do it. I don't work well in groups because I have to do everything myself.

161

BC: I understand there is an interesting story involving the Russian film-maker Sergei Eisenstein and a photograph of yours.

WESTON: There was a young man named Seymour Stern who was a radical young firebrand back in Hollywood in the early thirties. He was a friend of my father, twenty-five years old and a brilliant intellectual. I was nineteen. He had a little magazine called *Experimental Cinema* which is now defunct, of course, but he used to use some of my photographs of celebrities on the cover. One day Seymour asked if I'd like to photograph Eisenstein. I had seen his films and I said I'd love to.

He brought Eisenstein to my little place on Hollywood Boulevard along with Eisenstein's cameraman Eric Tisse. I was photographing him out on the patio when my friend Seymour began telling me that I must photograph him this way and that way—directing me—and Tisse got over my shoulder with his Leica and began photographing simultaneously. It was like a shooting gallery! Well today I would have said, gentlemen, can you get yourselves out of here for half an hour—in a nice way, of course—but then, as a young kid, I was intimidated. I told Seymour twenty years later, "I should have kicked your ass out of there."

Eisenstein was very nice, though. He was about thirty-five then with bushy hair and spoke broken English. He saw a few of my photographs lying around and suddenly declared, "I vant dat!" Without another word, he picked up my photograph of "Three Fingers And An Ear" and walked off with it. I couldn't stop him because I was intimidated, but it was a great compliment. That photograph later appeared on the cover of *Camera* magazine.

BC: Did Eisenstein have anything to do with that?

WESTON: No, no. They were doing a thing on the *f*/64 Group. *Camera* did a whole issue on *f*/64. I was not really part of the group but they had invited me to participate in the exhibition.

BC: What did you think of the f/64 Group at the time?

WESTON: I thought it was a good catalyst. I knew the people in it well: Imogen Cunningham, Ansel Adams, my father, and Willard Van Dyke. But Dad was never a joiner and he got out early. It only lasted about a year or so anyway. I was in Santa Barbara at the time and they invited me to show in a huge exhibit at the deYoung Museum when I was about twenty or twenty-one.

BC: Were you influenced by the work of Ansel Adams or Imogen Cunningham at the time?

WESTON: I don't think so. They are both very important people for various reasons. Besides being a great artist, Ansel has set a great example of craftsmanship. Imogen was not as great a craftsman—her work isn't that consistent—but she made a number of stunning memorable images in her long career.

BC: What do you think of Ansel Adams' Zone System?

WESTON: It's a gimmick for teachers who have to have something to talk about. The pamphlets and books on it are asinine to me.

Number one: if you're a full time photographer your memory and experience take over. You memorize light and develop such a feel for particular lighting conditions that you don't need a goddamned meter.

Number two: it gets in the way of creativity. All these notes are an impediment in the field and any old-time photographer who works continuously—if he's worth his salt—hasn't got time for gimmicks. He knows from experience and memory, which becomes instinct. I'm not saying there isn't a place for the Zone System with young students who haven't the time to understand light and its qualities, but I worked long before there were meters and before the Zone System was even heard of. With the Zone System you have to have adequate meters and your meter is synchronized to your shutter. Correct? Well, the shutters and meters are almost never the same. There's always a variation. It's a device for teaching but it isn't any good for me.

Ansel and I are very close friends. He didn't originate the Zone System, he just put a handle on it. It was being done by Mortensen and Laguna a long time ago. We were with a group of people once and Ansel had one of his apprentices there and Ansel turned to me and said, "You know, Brett, if you let Lillian teach you the Zone System, it might improve your work."

163

And I replied, "Ansel, most of the great photographs of all time were made without the Zone System." He didn't say a word.

I'm very harsh when it comes to criticism of other photographers' work and ideas. For example, I think almost all of Steichen's work was purely commercial and pretty shitty for the most part. It was a compromise. He was always pleasing some editor or some half-assed art director and the publisher. Steichen was a whore and a big bleeding Germanic heart. He was so full of bullshit, God! Museum of Modern Art, Madison Avenue. He was a very competent commercial hack fifty years ago. A big money-maker.

Stieglitz was more genuine and a great photographer. He was a promoter and the best thing he ever did was to promote Georgia O'Keeffe, his wife. He was dedicated to her.

I can be pretty volatile, pretty arrogant, and pretty opinionated about the work and the personalities of many photographers.

BC: As you know, Imogen Cunningham died last week. I was wondering if you could say a few words about her.

WESTON: She was marvelous. Caustic as hell. I knew Imogen from the time I was eight years old. I liked the old gal—a fabulous character—but in my opinion not a great artist.

BC: What in your opinion kept her from being a great photographer?

WESTON: It is hard to say. Maybe it was her abrasive personality. She was a kind of bleeding heart and a bit of a Parlor Pink— and she just didn't have a fierce enduring eye. She didn't go all-out. Some of her late work of people on the street was really pretty bad. I think she was overrated as a photographer, but she was a fantastic person. She was a poor technician and craftsman generally, but she did have a good eye and did a few very fine pictures. I'm being very honest.

BC: What did you think of Minor White's work? I understand you were friends.

WESTON: I have mixed reactions. Some stunning things and some not so good. He was primarily a teacher.

BC : How do you feel about Cartier-Bresson's work?

WESTON: Cartier-Bresson is not really a photographer—to me that is. He's a philosopher and a photojournalist but not a photographer. He can't print, for starters. He has someone do it for him. To me he is not a photographer in the sense that my father was, or Ansel Adams or myself are. He is more interested in the social scene.

BC : So the craft of printing is crucial in determining whether a person is a photographer or not?

WESTON: Of course. Whether you're writing or painting or photographing, craft is your vehicle. I think technique is terribly important.

BC : Who would you think has the highest quality in printing? Ansel Adams?

WESTON: He's a very fine craftsman, but there are many fine young people who do equally well technically. Seeing is the important thing. One's perceptions come first. Darkroom work is the continuation of what you saw in your ground glass. It is the completion, the finalization of the image seen on the back of the ground glass. Your final perception must be printed beautifully if it is going to be successful. That's what I have against Cartier-Bresson.

BC : Did you ever consider being a photojournalist?

WESTON: No. In the army I was briefly a photographer in the Signal Corps, but it didn't inspire me.

BC : I understand you had to go through basic training three times.

WESTON: Correct. I got myself out of the infantry and they put me in truck-driving. They had no place for my kind of photography.

BC : Had you used any small cameras at that point?

WESTON: Nothing smaller than a 4x5 Graflex.

BC: Have you used small cameras since then?

WESTON: The last nine years I've used the SL-66 Rollei and the RD Mamiya $2\frac{1}{4}$x$3\frac{3}{4}$. They are magnificently flexible but generally I use a small view camera on a tripod. I still use the 8x10 sporadically and for a twenty-year period I used an 11x14. A change of pace in cameras is a very healthy thing. A man needs a change.

BC: Do you think a certain vision requires a particular camera?

WESTON: I respect the 35mm; it was extremely important to the development of photojournalism, but it doesn't suit my temperament or the photography I do.

BC: What aspect of your personality made photojournalism unsuitable to you?

WESTON: I'm interested in humanity and all that, but the moment propaganda enters into art, it becomes a compromise. Unless you're a giant like Orozco or El Greco or Bach and can rise above it. I guess I just never got the message.

BC: Did you ever have any doubts about yourself as a photographer?

WESTON: Never. Supreme arrogance, complete love of my work, and absolute dedication.

BC: So a strong ego helped your photography?

WESTON: Of course! An artist has to have a strong ego. He has to be enamored of his work. His art has to be the most important thing in his life, whether he's a writer, a painter, or a photographer. He has to be pretty damned self-assured. I throw away a lot of my work, but that comes of a knowledge of my weak areas. You just tear it up and throw it out.

BC: Is this only recent work that you destroy if it doesn't meet the standard?

WESTON: No. I've destroyed stacks of old negatives and prints over the years. I've done this twice—just taken a third of my life's work and thrown it away. I still have an enormous body of work, though.

BC: Do you get appeals from art historians over this mass destruction?

WESTON: I couldn't care less about art historians. Why should they pore over my junk and then work it over? I'm a little concerned about posterity but my basic drive is to create, not to be famous.

BC: Do photographers talk about their work much with other photographers?

WESTON: They talk technique, I guess, but I'm kind of a loner. I don't get involved in other photographers' work. I have some very good friends who are photographers, but their work doesn't affect me very much. I'm more affected by painters or musicians or writers.

BC: Any particular ones?

WESTON: It is not a direct influence. I don't try to illustrate music, for example. It's just a very subtle feeling. I'm probably unaware of it. But I love the work of painters like Charles Sheeler, Georgia O'Keeffe, and some Picasso and Modigliani. I'm sure I've been influenced by the Japanese and by the French writers—that is, my spirit has been influenced.

BC: Are you at all interested in Zen or Eastern philosophies?

WESTON: No. I don't respond to regimentation of any kind in religions.

BC: One of your best-known photographs is of a Japanese tombstone covered with a pattern of lichen so that the characters were ghostly and mysterious. Did you mean anything symbolic in it?

WESTON: No. I was merely responding to visual beauty. It was a lovely thing so I isolated it and photographed it. I don't think in terms of Minor's theories at all. That business just bores the hell out of me, that philosophy.

BC : Do you feel that details of reality taken out of their context and enlarged take on a surreal or symbolic nature?

WESTON: Look, it's a visual medium. I'm just a photographer. I'm the wrong person to ask.

BC : Is a photograph successful if it cannot be explained verbally because in this way it remains purely visual?

WESTON: I don't try to define my work verbally at all. I can do it speaking about technique but not on aesthetics. I had no formal training and I'm not much on formal verbiage or slide-rule art. This verbal gobbledy-gook just bores the hell out of me, I'm sorry. It might excite certain pseudo-intellectuals but it doesn't excite me. All this art talk on painting and photography is a pile of horseshit. Most critics don't know what they're talking about—they're just writing for their bread and butter. I have great respect for writing—certain writers—and conversation, but all my effort goes into making photographs, not talking about them. I sound off occasionally, like now, but I don't like to intellectualize. I have no secrets. I like to share what technical knowledge I have with young people, but beyond that I have little to say to them except for encouragement if it is appropriate. I can't explain something that is just a matter of seeing.

BC : Do you find any similarity between your work and Aaron Siskind's?

WESTON: Not remotely. We both photograph "crud," but to me he has a more painterly eye. He is a fine photographer but he might have been an even finer painter. Strangely enough, Ansel said the same thing about my work.

BC : Do you see your work falling into distinct periods?

WESTON: To begin with, I didn't really go through a "developmental" period as a young photographer. I think I was born with a perceptive eye that was immediately attracted to the clarity of the direct photograph. My perceptions have changed over the years, to be sure, and I've photographed many different things in this world, but it is hard for me to pinpoint any big breaks in my career. My work today is more complex in composition and more assured.

BC: What years do you consider your best work?

WESTON: My present work. You move ahead. You don't rest on your laurels.

BC: Is there one picture of yours that stands out as your favorite?

WESTON: No. My work is too varied. I have maybe 500 favorites from many countries and many periods. I have two or three thousand photographs that I consider good enough to leave around when I die.

BC: Do you shoot every day?

WESTON: No, but I'm immersed in some aspect of photography every day: either printing, spotting, mounting or talking photography (I shout and curse now and then in the darkroom).

BC: How long does it take you to photograph something?

WESTON: Once I've seen it, I expose very quickly. Not the way Cartier-Bresson would—shooting from the hip—because my work is different. Paul Strand used to spend hours on one thing but I see very quickly. I use cumbersome tripods and cameras but once you master these, you can work very rapidly and precisely.

BC: Do you find that you see photographically even when you are not working?

WESTON: My eye is always wandering and seeking. Always alert, instinctively. It's not something you can turn off.

BC: What do you feel at the precise instant you press the shutter release?

WESTON: Great excitement. My father used to call it a climax of emotion.

BC: How long are your exposures generally?

WESTON: They run the gamut from $\frac{1}{25}$ of a second to 10 minutes.

BC: *When would you use ten minutes?*

WESTON: In a very dark area, stopped down completely.

BC: *You mentioned earlier that you didn't use a light meter when photographing.*

WESTON: That's true, unless I change film or I'm hung over or just lazy.

I don't bracket, though.* Not with a big camera anyway—with a small one I do just in case there's a problem with the roll of film.

BC: *Have you ever staged a photograph in nature?*

WESTON: I did occasionally when I was a child and I would do it today, but generally things are more exciting when they're found. Every time you move your camera or lower your tripod you are arranging or re-staging a photograph. My father arranged his still-lifes of cabbage leaves and those amazing shells, but I usually don't.

BC: *I meant if you saw a composition in some kelp that interested you but didn't quite make it, would you move a strand into alignment?*

WESTON: Generally not, because then you disturb the elegance and the beauty of what you've found.

BC: *Does photography impose an unnatural order over nature or do you think of photography as a natural phenomenon?*

WESTON: Photography is man-made and a creation of science, so in that sense it is unnatural, but so is a piano or a violin and television.

BC: *What is it about nature that makes you want to photograph it?*

---

*Bracketing is a photographer's term for making two or more exposures of the same subject, often at slightly different settings, to be sure of getting a correctly exposed negative.

WESTON: Nature is a great artist. The greatest. I've seen rocks and forms that put Matisse and Picasso and Brancusi to shame. You can't beat Mother Nature. The thing that amazed me was realizing that I could capture this in a second with my eye and camera. The vision controls the tool. That's why I'm down on the school of photography that feels they have to alter the integrity of the photographic image. Why don't these people take up painting? Somehow, cutting up a photograph for a collage doesn't ring true to me. It's all this trying for something new, trying to be different. You don't try to be different, you simply *are* different.

BC: So artists or photographers are born with a different vision?

WESTON: If they aren't, they'd better throw away their paintbrushes and cameras.

BC: You often photograph objects that have been damaged or scarred by time and the elements. How do you explain this beyond just a visual curiosity?

WESTON: The taint of age can be very beautiful. The wreckage of man-made objects is sometimes more beautiful than the new. Rust and weathering adds a patina of . . . well, I call it "elegant shit" or "elegant gorp."

BC: Has the medium of photography redefined the idea of beauty distinct from painting?

WESTON: Like anyone else, I think something of flawless beauty is marvelous, but imperfection and irregularity can be equally stunning when captured by the photographic image. What is disturbing is to see the uniqueness of the medium mongrelized by the mixing of media, bizarre retouching and alteration. Why butcher it? I'm a purist in this sense.

BC: What are the weaknesses of photography?

WESTON: It's so easy, or rather people are under the illusion or misconception that it's easy. Well, I could teach a two-year-old child to push a button and he'd come up with some kind of image. It is difficult to do it superbly, though. Technically it is complex. You have a million options with equipment to distract you. I tell my students to simplify their equipment.

BC : What are the strengths of photography?

WESTON: It can do something no other thing can do. It can record beauty precisely in a split second. A painter can't do this, a writer can't do this, a sculptor can't do this.

BC : Could you describe your habits in the darkroom?

WESTON: I always work standing up, never sitting. I work in silence except for the noise of the timer lights, the voltage regulator and the noises of the water flowing. I don't like music in the darkroom the way my brother Cole does and I don't use a metronome. Ansel has one going click, click, click the whole time like the Pit and the Pendulum. I kid him about it, but it would drive me nuts. I usually get up before dawn and work from three to five hours.

BC : How much darkroom manipulation do you do?

WESTON: Minimal. I don't do any superimposing or double exposures except by accident once or twice and these have been tragedies. The multiple-exposure work of Jerry Uelsmann is nothing new. It's just a fad that has caught on. It was done better fifty years ago by the Bauhaus School. It is a gimmick that only comes off once in a while.

BC : Do you retouch your photographs?

WESTON: No, only when as a young man I had to in the portrait business. Now I will still take out a minor blemish or dust speck on the negative. I spot the prints, but I don't like to impose anything foreign on the photographic image.

BC : How do you feel about the quality of reproduction being done today for photography books?

WESTON: I think it has improved a great deal. My recent book by Aperture* is very well done, but my next book is going to

*A Voyage of the Eye.

have no titles, no poetry or text, and no foreword—just a series of photographs. No ballyhoo or bullshit. The history of photography has never interested me.

BC: Do different photographers have problems reproducing their work because of the particular type of photographs they make?

WESTON: I don't follow these things very closely. Some photographers do print their work in a special way to take into account the way the prints will be reproduced. Ansel Adams works very closely with his printers and has contributed a great deal to the art of reproduction.

BC: But you're not interested in reproduction.

WESTON: No. I'm more interested in the photograph as an object. Photographers like Stieglitz and Paul Strand experimented with gravures, but I prefer the photographic image to the one reproduced in ink.

BC: How do you prefer your work exhibited?

WESTON: A simple presentation. Not too many photographs, well-spaced. Good lighting is very important.

BC: What kind of response do you hope to elicit from your audience?

WESTON: I love an audience, we all do, but I'd rather have an audience of say a thousand people who really love my work than ten million—in general mass audiences are tasteless. I'd rather have a select audience who understood my work and appreciated it. Usually the people who like my work are photographers, scientists, painters, writers, but sometimes I'll find a very simple man who is a bricklayer or carpenter who will respond to my work and I love this. I've found from shows in Mexico that the Latin audience, curiously enough, seemed more sensitive artistically than our society. I've had over a hundred one-man shows. It's very satisfying.

BC: How do you deal with criticism?

WESTON: It goes in one ear and out the other. The press comes up with the worst kind of poppycock and I've been ignoring it for forty-five years. For the most part it is distorted, inaccurate and badly written. I've had a lot of applause and been shredded by a few people like Margery Mann, but then she shreds everyone unless you're a bleeding heart. She's a third-rate photographer-turned-critic and she doesn't know her ass from a hot rock. She's ripped up Ansel Adams, Edward Weston and me for years. She said we've done too many rocks. Well, I agree that I've done too many rocks, but there's also been too many badly done ash-can type pictures of bleeding hearts and Negroes which she loves. I'm sick of that sociology.

BC: *Would you say a photographer's choice of subject matter reflects some significant aspect of his personality?*

WESTON: Very much so.

BC: *Is it possible that the photographer is unaware of the aspect of himself that he is expressing? Is the visual so based in instinct that it defies analysis?*

WESTON: With me it is. Look, I'm just a photographer and I love to photograph. I have a very strong sense of form and design and beauty. It's built in. If my work doesn't show these three things, then I throw it in the trash can. I'm not interested in cute sexual symbolisms or the ash-can school or sociology. I don't do propaganda with the camera, or at least I don't do it purposely.

BC: *So you don't see any deep Freudian concepts lurking behind your motivation for photographing?*

WESTON: For me it is a fulfilment. My work is my philosophy, my life, and my way of life. Four marriages and chasing girls fits in there, too, but photography has been my life.

BC: *Do you see anything destructive in some attitudes that are being developed in the photography world?*

WESTON: If these young photographers really have it, they couldn't care less what is going on. If they really have it. Not many people do, of any age.

BC : So you don't see photography as a disappearing frontier?

WESTON: It's still wide open. If you have the imagination and the heart and the vision. Just forget what other people are doing.